SUV RVing

How to Travel, Camp, Sleep, Explore, and Thrive in the Ultimate Tiny House

By Tristan Higbee

Copyright © 2016 by Tristan Higbee. All rights reserved.

This book or any portion thereof may not be reproduced or used in any manner whatsoever without the express written permission of the author except for the use of brief quotations in a review.

All images are by the author unless otherwise noted.

Cover photo: The author's SUV parked for the night (for free!) in southern Utah's Valley of the Gods.

Visit the author's website at *http://SUVRVing.com*.

DISCLAIMER
The information in this book is for educational purposes only. Sleeping in your vehicle can be illegal and/or dangerous. Check all local laws and use common sense before implementing anything you read in this book. The author will not be held responsible for anything you do regarding traveling, sleeping, or living in a vehicle. Follow the advice here at your own risk. Please be safe out there.

Contents

1. An Introduction to SUV RVing — 1

Who is SUV RVing for? — 1
Why an SUV? — 2
Why not an SUV? — 3
What makes for a good SUV RV? — 3
My SUV RVing story — 4

2. Sleeping — 6

The sleeping area — 6
Bed comfort — 17
Privacy — 19
Temperature — 25
- Staying cool in hot weather — 25
- Staying warm in cold weather — 29

Other sleep tips — 31

3. Storage — 33

Take less stuff — 33
On-seat and on-floor storage — 34
Compartment storage — 34
Gap storage — 39
Organizers and aftermarket vehicle storage — 39
Bins, boxes, and bags — 42
Hanging things — 43
Under-platform storage — 45
The rear shelf — 45
Built-ins — 48
The roof — 48
The front — 51
The back — 51
Trailers — 52
Organization and clutter — 53

4. What to Take With You — 54

Clothing — 54
Navigation — 55
Sleeping — 56

Electronics	57
Vehicle stuff	57
Camping gear	57
Tools, etc.	58
Toiletries, etc.	58
Cooking, etc.	58
Emergencies/Safety	59
Other stuff	59
Final words on packing	59

5. Where to Camp — 61

BLM land	61
National forests	64
Other public lands	66
Public campgrounds	66
Private campgrounds and RV parks	67
Truck stops	68
Walmart parking lots	68
Other parking lots	68
Street parking	69
Other places to camp	69
Tips and best practices of urban/suburban camping	70
Leave no trace	71

6. Food and Cooking — 74

Refrigeration	74
Going stoveless	75
Cooking	79
• Where to cook	79
• Stoves	82
• Unconventional cooking methods	85
• My kitchen items	85
• What to cook	85
• Cleaning the cookware and utensils	88
Water	90

7. Toilets and Bathing — 92

Going to the bathroom	92
• Public facilities	92
• Portable flush toilets	93
• Portable non-flush toilets	93
• Non-toilets	96

- Portable toilets and privacy 97
Keeping clean 98
  - Showering 98
  - Powered portable showers 99
  - Gravity showers 101
  - Dirtbag showers 102
  - Miscellaneous shower thoughts and tips 103

8. Electronics and Internet Access 104

Powering electronic devices 104
  - Power inverters 104
  - House batteries 107
  - USB-powered devices 109
  - Generators 110
  - Charging devices elsewhere 111
Useful electronic devices 111
Cable management 112
The hanging laptop desk 113
Useful smartphone apps 114
Internet access 114

9. Keeping the SUV Clean 117

The outside 117
The inside 117
  - Mats, covers, etc. 117
  - Cleanliness 119
  - Dealing with trash 120

10. What to See and Do 122

What to see 122
Resources 125
Hobbies 126

11. Safety and Security 128

Getting stuck or stranded 129
Weapons 131
Emergencies 131
Weather 133
Emergency communication 134
Theft and break-ins 135
Cameras 136

12. Long-Term SUV RVing — 138

Outdoor living areas — 138
Indoor living areas — 143
Temporary home bases — 144
Doing laundry — 144
Staying healthy — 146
Other stuff — 147

Endnotes — 149
About the author — 150
Other books by the author — 150

1. An Introduction to SUV RVing

SUV RVing is exactly what it sounds like: traveling, sleeping, and doing other things that you'd do in an RV (recreational vehicle) but in an SUV (sport utility vehicle). By day it's visiting family and friends, seeing national parks, enjoying the outdoors, getting from Point A to Point B, or just getting away from it all. By night it's sleeping in comfortable campgrounds, remote forests, empty deserts, vibrant cities—wherever you want. It's the freedom and flexibility of an RV with the maneuverability, efficiency, low profile, and low price tag of an SUV. Whether you're going on a short trip and just need to spend one night in your vehicle or are living out of your SUV full-time, you'll find useful and valuable information in this book.

Though this book was written from the standpoint of an American SUV RVer and some things will pertain only to North America, much of what is written here is applicable all over the world.

And while I talk specifically about SUVs because that's what I have personal experience with, the majority of this book can also be applied to traveling and sleeping in a van, truck, car, or RV. In other words, if you're thinking about life on the road, this book is for you.

Who is SUV RVing for?

It's for anyone who wants to travel inexpensively.

It's for anyone who can't afford, doesn't want to pay for, doesn't have the room to store, and/or doesn't want to drive a traditional RV.

It's for anyone who wants to be nomadic.

It's for anyone who wants to experience a simpler life.

It's for anyone who likes to camp but doesn't like messing around with setting up and taking down tents.

It's for weekend warriors, overnighters, spring breakers, and people without a home.

It's for people who long for the "vandwelling" or "#vanlife" lifestyles but don't have or want to get a van.

It's for anyone who, for whatever reason, chooses or is forced to sleep in their vehicle.

It's for anyone who wants a small vacation home on wheels.

It's for anyone who wants to experience the ultimate "tiny house" lifestyle.

Why an SUV?

So why travel around in an SUV versus some other type of vehicle? Why not a van or a "real" RV? Why not just camp in a tent or get a motel room?

There are pros and cons to each of these methods of travel and lodging. One of the biggest benefits of SUV RVing is that a lot of us already have SUVs. We don't need to spend the money on a new vehicle. RVing in the SUV you already own is the cheapest way to get out and explore. If you are looking to buy a vehicle, SUVs come in a wide variety of shapes, sizes, and styles for a variety of budgets, so you'll be able to find a vehicle that works perfectly for you.

Another benefit of traveling around in SUVs is that they can go a lot of places other vehicles can't. You certainly couldn't and wouldn't want to take that shiny $150,000 motorhome onto a sandy Forest Service road or rocky desert track. I've taken my SUV on some really rough four-wheel-drive roads that would eat most vans alive. They nearly ate my SUV alive, but the upshot was that I've been able to access some amazing areas and have them all to myself. And unlike that fancy motorhome or even a good-sized camper van, any SUV will be able to fit just fine into standard parking spots found in any parking lot, from the Walmart in town to the small pullout on the side of the road to the busy parking lots of Yosemite or Yellowstone on Labor Day weekend. Moreover, your average SUV will get much better gas mileage than your average conventional RV—I get up to 31 miles per gallon in mine. That means more money in my pocket for more adventures. No more taking out a second mortgage just to get to where you're going.

For years I hated camping. I did it more out of necessity than desire. I camped because I'm an avid rock climber, and the things I wanted to climb were out in the middle of nowhere, so camping was the only option. The problem was that my camping experiences all involved setting up and taking down a tent, something that I despise. These are especially onerous tasks in the rain. There is nothing worse than wrestling with a big ball of wet nylon, getting soaked in the process, and unavoidably bringing some of the rain inside the tent. I've found that it's so much easier and more comfortable to sleep in my SUV. It's also much less fragile. I don't worry about strong winds blowing down my shelter in the middle of the night.

The average cost of a hotel room in the United States is $137 per night.[1] I've spent about 30 nights in my SUV in the last few months, meaning that I've saved more than $4,000 by sleeping in my vehicle. That's enough to buy a nice used vehicle in the first place!

SUVs really do provide the best of all worlds. They're more rugged and capable than your average van or RV. They're more economical than conventional recreational vehicles and hotels. And they make camping so much easier, more enjoyable, and less stressful.

Why *not* an SUV?

Though I believe that SUV RVing is a great option for many people, it's not always the best option. The biggest downside is space. If you need or want a lot of space inside your home on wheels, an SUV might not be what you're looking for. Even a standard-sized minivan will feel larger than a big SUV. I can imagine two adults and a child (maybe two children if they are small and the SUV is large) sleeping in an SUV, but it's not ideal for a family. Having said that, the small interior does not bother me as a single individual. I take it as an exercise in minimalism, as a challenge to reexamine what I have around me and take only what I need. An SUV is the ultimate movable tiny house, but very tiny houses aren't for everyone.

One downside of an SUV compared to a larger RV is that you won't be able to take advantage of all the hookups that are available at RV parks or campgrounds around the country (i.e., water, sewer, and electricity) in the same way you would in a traditional RV. If you want a facsimile of your house on wheels, an SUV isn't for you. You're not going to have an indoor shower, flushing toilet, big-screen TV, or multiple rooms. SUV RVing is more like camping, but it is much more comfortable than traditional tent camping.

What makes for a good SUV RV?

I bought my SUV knowing that I would be traveling and sleeping in it a lot, and I kept two big things in mind when looking at different vehicles. These are things that anyone who doesn't already have an SUV might also want to keep in mind, although what is important to me may be different from what is important to you.

First, I wanted a vehicle that would get decent gas mileage. I wanted to cover a lot of ground and not have to break the bank to do it. I wanted to be able to drive places even when gas prices were high, and if I wanted to go on an adventure somewhere, I didn't want the cost of getting there to play heavily into the equation.

Second, I wanted to be able to sleep in the vehicle without having to do any major modifications. In other words, I wanted to be able to sleep in the SUV without having to remove seats or build a sleeping platform. The easier it was to get from a normal setup to a sleeping setup, the better. Most of the SUVs I looked at had rear seats that would fold forward to create a larger cargo area in the back, which was great and what I wanted, but not all of these folded-down seats made for a good sleeping area. Some didn't lay down all the way flat. Others created weird bumps or ridges that would make sleeping extremely uncomfortable, if even possible. Others didn't create a cargo/sleeping area long enough for me (and yes, I kept folding down the rear seats and crawling into the back of many SUVs at the car dealerships).

There are several other factors to keep in mind when on the hunt for an

SUV to travel and sleep in. I didn't mention reliability as one of my two most important factors because that's a given. Of course I want a reliable vehicle. High clearance (which most SUVs already have) and four-wheel drive come in handy if you want to go off the beaten track. Interior space is definitely something else to be aware of. My Toyota RAV4 is certainly on the smaller end of the SUV spectrum, but it's got all the space I need and more. Space relates not only to how much room you and your traveling companions will have to sleep in but how much room you'll have for your stuff and how big of a vehicle you're willing to drive. Engine size and power are also things to consider if you want to do serious off-roading or want to tow something behind your SUV, but be aware that a larger engine will negatively affect fuel efficiency. Finally, a sunroof is great for ventilation and would be a nice thing to have in any SUV you plan on sleeping in.

My SUV RVing story

My first vehicle was a 1996 Plymouth Breeze. If you are unfamiliar with that make and model of car, just picture in your mind a small and conventional four-door sedan. That's pretty much what my Breeze was. I drove that vehicle all around the American West as I hiked, climbed, scaled mountains, and explored national parks. It was a good car for me at the time, but I realized during those adventures that things would have been so much easier if I could have just slept in the car. While it was technically possible to sleep in my Breeze by just leaning the front seats as far back as they would go, it was terribly uncomfortable. The same is true for most vehicles.

Travel and the freedom to do what I want have always been important to me, and it was as I traveled around the western US that I realized I had too much stuff, or more precisely, that I didn't need all that I had back at home. Over the course of about six months, I sold or gave away nearly everything I owned. Everything that remained could easily fit in the trunk of the Breeze. With my newfound flexibility and the freedom of not having things to tie me down, I sold the Breeze to a friend, put a single bag of climbing and camping gear in storage, and flew to Mexico with a one-way ticket and one carry-on bag. I spent the next three years living in and traveling through Mexico, Eastern Europe, Southeast Asia, and South Asia. It was glorious, and I had no problem living with just what I could carry on my back.

When I came back to America, it was time to buy a new vehicle, and I knew I wanted one that I could sleep in. I considered everything from a Prius to a cargo van but eventually decided on a small SUV (the aforementioned Toyota RAV4). The SUV gets great gas mileage (about 22 miles per gallon in the city and 31 miles per gallon when going 60 miles per hour on highways), has relatively high clearance (compared to a Prius or minivan), and is very easy to convert from a normal passenger vehicle to camping vehicle by simply folding down the back seats.

Since getting my SUV, I've traveled to 16 national parks, 18 national monuments, and countless cities in nine states (and those are big states in the western US!). I fell in love with the simple freedom of driving, exploring, sleeping, and doing it all over again the next day.

When first trying to figure out how to best travel and sleep in my SUV, I was surprised and a bit frustrated by the lack of quality information available. After figuring everything out on my own, I decided to take all of my hard-earned knowledge and package it for other would-be SUV RVers so they could avoid my expensive and time-consuming mistakes. This book is the result of my experiences and a whole lot of trial and error.

Note: Due to the fact that web addresses change and products come onto and then go off of the market, I've tried to keep mentions of (and links to) specific products or websites within this book to a minimum. Instead, I've listed many relevant products, links, and other supplementary material for each chapter on the book's website (http://suvrving.com/book), which is easier to keep updated. A link to the page for each chapter will be included at the beginning of each of the following chapters.

2. Sleeping

To see additional relevant links for this chapter, visit http://suvrving.com/book/two/.

Sleeping is the first thing that comes to mind when people think about using an SUV as an RV. Is it doable? Is it comfortable? Yes and yes. There are four elements that work together to make your SUV sleeping experience a good one: the sleeping area, bed comfort, privacy, and temperature. By controlling these factors, you can make sure that your SUV sleeping experience is a good one.

The sleeping area

The basic idea of sleeping in any SUV is that you either remove or fold down the rear row(s) of seats and then create some sort of bed in the back behind the front seats. If you were to chop off the roof of an SUV with a bed inside and look down on it, it might look as shown in Figure 1.

In the perfect SUV, the rear row(s) of seats would fold from an upright position down to a completely flat surface behind the front seats. (See Figures 2 and 3.)

It is on this generally level area that you would put a mattress and gear. Ideally, going from a normal seating configuration in your SUV to a sleeping configuration would be as simple as pulling a lever or two to fold down the rear seats.

Most SUVs are not perfect, however, and it's more likely that your SUV falls into one of the following three categories:

1. The rear row(s) of seats fold(s) down at a steep angle, creating a sleeping platform that is not completely level. (See Figure 4.)

2. The rear row(s) of seats fold(s) down but the headrests or other parts of the seat create bumps or bulges that would push into your back or neck. (See Figure 5.) Removing the headrests (if possible) may solve the problem.

3. The rear row(s) of seats fold(s) down but do not sit close to flush with the floor of the rear cargo area. (See Figure 6.)

An option with the configuration as shown in Figure 6 is to remove the rear seats entirely and store them elsewhere, leaving you with a larger, more or less flat surface. (See Figure 7.)

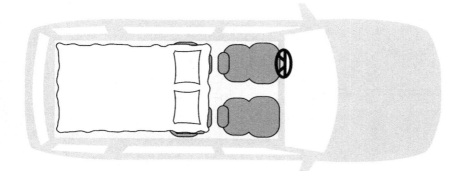

Figure 1. Illustration of a top-down view of an SUV with the rear seat area leveled and a bed with pillows in place

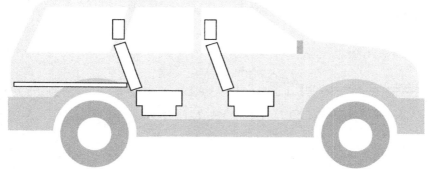

Figure 2. Illustration of a side view of an SUV with the rear seats upright and in passenger mode

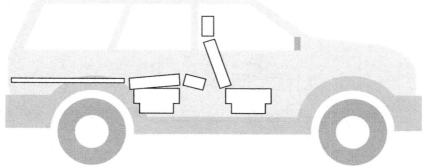

Figure 3. Illustration of a side view of an SUV with the rear seats folded forward to create a sleeping area. While the rear seats may not fold down to create a perfectly level sleeping surface, a good mattress can make up for the differences.

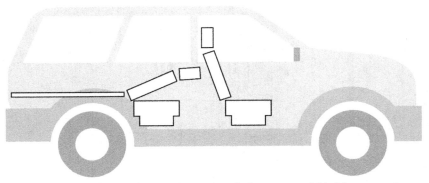

Figure 4. Illustration of a side view of an SUV with the rear seats folded down at a steep angle

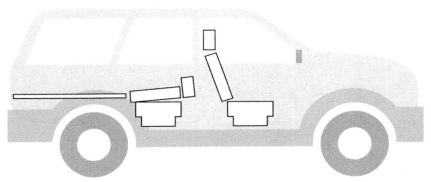

Figure 5. Illustration of a side view of an SUV with the rear seats folded down to create an uncomfortable bump or bulge

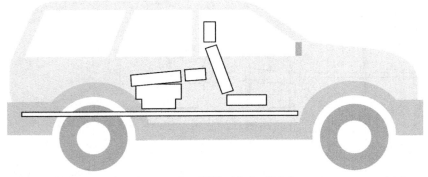

Figure 6. Illustration of a side view of an SUV with the folded rear seat on a completely different level from the cargo area

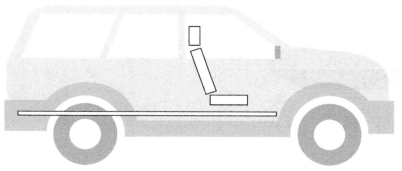

Figure 7. Illustration of a side view of an SUV with the rear row(s) of seats removed

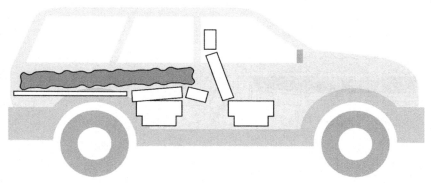

Figure 8. The rear seats folded down almost completely flat, leaving no gap space that needs to be filled

Regardless of the layout of your SUV, there's a good chance that the rear area will still need to be leveled out a bit in order to create a comfortable sleeping platform. Broadly speaking, there are two approaches you can take here: filling in the gaps and building a platform.

Filling in the gaps involves building up low areas to make them higher, as shown in the five examples illustrated in Figures 8–12. In these examples, the dark gray shape with wavy edges is the bed or mattress, and the black area represents the gap space that needs to be filled. The first image (Figure 8) shows the setup with the seats that fold down almost completely flat, so there is no significant gap space that needs to be filled.

Regardless of the layout of your SUV, there's a good chance that the rear area will still need to be leveled out a bit in order to create a comfortable sleeping platform. Broadly speaking, there are two approaches you can take here: filling in the gaps and building a platform.

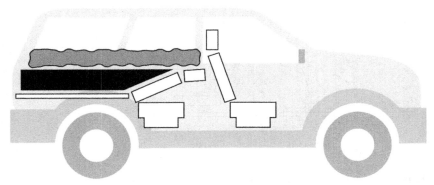

Figure 9. The rear seats folded down at a steep angle, leaving the black gap space that needs to be filled

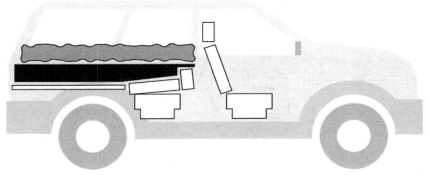

Figure 10. The rear seats folded down to create a bump or bulge, leaving the black gap space that needs to be filled

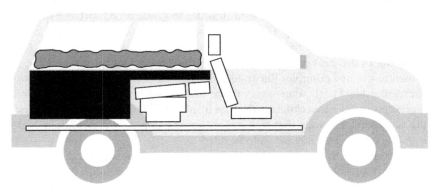

Figure 11. The rear seats folded down to create an uneven surface, leaving the black gap space to be filled

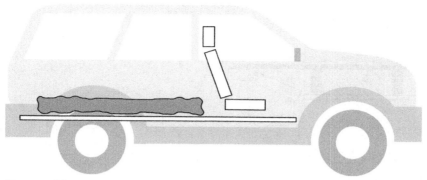

Figure 12. The rear seats removed completely, leaving no space that needs to be filled

Filling in the gaps involves building up low areas to make them higher, as shown in the five examples illustrated in Figures 8–12. In these examples, the dark gray shape with wavy edges is the bed or mattress, and the black area represents the gap space that needs to be filled. The first image (Figure 8) shows the setup with the seats that fold down almost completely flat, so there is no significant gap space that needs to be filled.

Building up the low areas can be done with bins, boxes, coolers, bags, quilts, mattress toppers, or other items you will be taking with you. Your mattress and other bedding materials then go on top of everything. The benefits of this filling-in-the-gaps setup are that (1) it can be done relatively inexpensively and without any tools, and (2) it is not permanent or even semi-permanent (i.e., it is easy to deploy and remove). The downsides are that (1) it may be hard to get your sleeping surface completely level, and (2) when you do need to access your stuff, you'll have to move the mattress that's sitting on top. If you're struggling with creating a uniformly flat surface, you may need to put a piece of plywood cut to fit the size of your mattress on top of the bins, boxes, bags, etc.

The second strategy for building a comfortable sleeping space is building a platform. This involves creating a solid platform that goes over all rear seats and all equipment, as illustrated in Figures 13–16 with the various rear seat styles. The solid black part in the illustrations represents the platform and supporting legs. In reality, more legs or other supports may be needed for your platform, but all are shown below with just a pair of legs in the front or middle and a pair in the back. Headroom is at a premium in most SUVs, and this will be especially true if you build a platform. Ideally, you'd want to be able to sit upright on your bed and not hit your head on the ceiling, but this may not be possible.

Think of building a platform as building a table that takes up all or most of the back of your SUV (depending on the size of the bed and SUV). The rear seats and whatever bins, bags, or other items you have all go under the table (some people also like to build slide-out drawers under their platforms), and your mattress and bedding go on top of the sleeping table. The surfaces of most

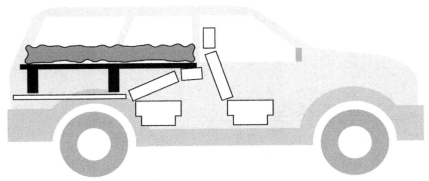

Figure 13. A platform over rear seats that fold down at a steep angle

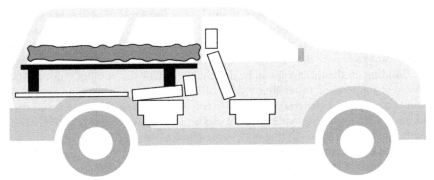

Figure 14. A platform over rear seats that fold down to create a bulge or bump

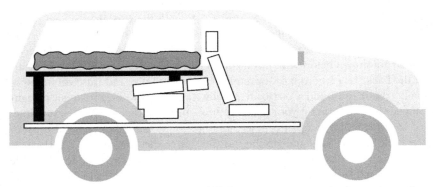

Figure 15. A platform over rear seats that fold down to create a completely uneven surface

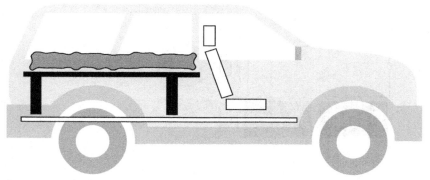

Figure 16. A platform built in the back of an SUV that has had all rear rows of seats completely removed

of the "tables" I've seen are made of ½-inch- or ¾-inch-thick plywood with vertical legs cut to the appropriate lengths from 2-inch by 4-inch (2x4) lumber. Horizontal 2x4 supports run underneath the plywood surface in the middle and at each end to add rigidity as necessary, although these may not be necessary with thicker plywood. The table should be put together with long screws rather than nails. With time and usage, nails will work their way loose. Long screws will not. You can purchase the plywood and 2x4 materials at a local building supply store. The helpful sales personnel at the store will usually cut the plywood to the dimensions you specify for free or a nominal per-cut fee. Borrow or buy an inexpensive hand saw to cut the 2x4 pieces to length. When choosing lumber, examine each piece to make sure that it is as straight as possible; many pieces for sale are not very straight.

I've also seen people use PVC pipes and galvanized steel pipes to create the legs and support braces. To give the platform a nicer, more finished look, many people will either paint/stain the platform or cover it in carpet. For some SUVs, a final approach to creating a comfortable sleeping area is a combination of filling in the gaps and building a platform.

Keep in mind that your setup doesn't have to take up the full width of your SUV. Because I usually travel and sleep alone in my SUV, I can use half of the width of the back of my SUV for my mattress and half for storage. (See Figure 17.)

If you want or need more room to stretch out when laying down, move the front seats as far forward as possible. Depending on the vehicle and your setup, this may result in a gap between the back of the front seats and the top of the folded-down rear seats. (See Figure 18.)

If you were to leave this gap as is, it might result in your head and mattress dropping down into this space. There are a couple of things that can be done to remedy this. The first is to fill that space with stuff—bins, boxes, clothing, bags, a cooler, etc. I sometimes use plastic bins to fill the gap. (See Figure 19.)

The second way of solving the gap dilemma is to build a platform that hangs

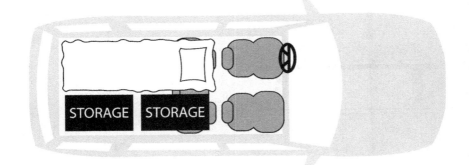

Figure 17. Illustration of a top-down view of an SUV sleeping and storage arrangement for one person

Figure 18. The gap between the back of the front seat and top of the folded-down rear seat

from the headrest of the front seat. (See Figure 20.) I made one from a thin sheet of plywood (cut for me to the right size in the home improvement store I bought it from), some paracord, and two carabiner keychains.

Either one of these two solutions (filling in the gap and bridging the gap) will work great. I personally prefer the hanging platform because using it avoids having to shuffle the bins around when I need to get stuff out of them.

I've also realized that due to the rigidity of my air mattress when fully

Figure 19. Plastic storage bins filling the gap between back of the front seat and top of the folded-down rear seat

Figure 20. Filling the gap between the folded-down rear seat and the front seat with a hanging platform made from a sheet of thin plywood

inflated, I don't actually need additional support for my head when I'm sleeping. But the extra support is still nice to have, especially when I sit upright in the sleeping area with my back up against the back of the front seat.

One bed/sleeping option that I need to mention that is very different from the others is a rooftop tent. These tents are stored and deployed on top of the vehicle. The base of the tent is a flat platform that makes sleeping possible, and most of these tents can be set up relatively quickly and easily compared to a conventional tent (e.g., you don't have to thread poles through loops of fabric or anything like that). The main benefits of these rooftop tents are that your sleeping space doesn't take up any space inside the SUV, you can park in rocky or brushy areas and not have to worry about finding a level place on which to pitch a normal tent, and no major modifications need to be done to the vehicle. And even if you do modify the inside of your SUV for sleeping, adding a rooftop tent is like adding on another room for more people. The downsides are that these things are not cheap (they start at around $900 and go upwards of $4,000) and are not practical if you're interested in sleeping in places like parking lots without being noticed. They also adversely affect gas mileage and prevent you from using the roof for extra storage. In addition, they may not be quite as safe as sleeping inside your vehicle. A tent can easily be entered by two- or four-footed predators, though of course having the tent on top of an SUV makes this a bit more difficult. If a threat arises at night when you are sleeping inside your locked vehicle, you can move from your bed to the driver's seat, start the vehicle, and drive off. If you are in a tent, you would be exposed to any predator between the time you exit your tent and enter your vehicle. The likelihood of something bad like that happening is very low, but it is something to consider.

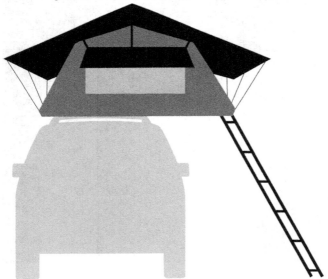

Figure 21. An example of a rooftop tent

Similar to the rooftop tent is another sleeping/shelter option, and that is a tent or shelter made to attach to the back or side of an opened SUV. An online search for "SUV tent" will bring up several commercially available freestanding tents that have a large fabric sleeve or tube on one side that slides over the rear end of an open SUV, effectively opening up the inside of the SUV to the inside of an extra room. The downside with these is that they are quite large and bulky when packed, so they would take up a lot of room inside an SUV.

There are also tents made to attach to the side of a vehicle. These are usually extra attachments that connect to awnings made by the same company (ARB, for example), but they can also be standalone tents. The main upside to these two related tent options is that they increase the amount of living space you have. The main downsides are that they are expensive to buy and time-consuming (and, arguably, unpleasant) to set up.

Finally, one of the simplest ways to add more interior space to your setup is to simply bring along a regular tent and pitch it next to your vehicle.

Bed comfort

Once you've got your sleeping platform and area worked out, it's time to think about what cushy material you'll be sleeping on. Bed options include the following:

- Air mattresses made specifically for SUVs
- Air mattresses made for camping or in-home use
- Lightweight foam or semi-inflatable sleeping pads made for camping
- Yoga mats
- Foam mattresses
- Foam mattress toppers
- Folded quilts or comforters
- Futon mattresses
- Cots – Because most cots have no insulation, you'll likely still want some sort of foam pad or other insulating material under you on cold nights.

If you're brave and/or have a high enough pain threshold, I suppose you could sleep without any source of padding, though one night of sleeping like that will probably convince you to do otherwise on your second night out.

Each type of bed or mattress has its pros and cons. Air mattresses pack up small and can be comfortable but are not very good insulators against cold and are best used in warmer weather. The thin foam backpacking sleeping pads or yoga mats are inexpensive but may not be thick enough to cover up any irregularities of your sleeping platform. Foam mattresses are warm and comfortable but bulky.

One thing that may or may not be important to you is how easy it is to pack up your bed. If you plan on having your bed laid out in the back of your SUV most of the time and rarely putting it away, the ease or difficulty of packing it up and then setting it up again isn't an issue. If you do plan to pack and unpack your bed often, something like an air mattress or camping mattress will be much less bulky when stowed than a futon or other thick mattress.

Another thing to consider is the size of your bed or mattress. If your SUV RV sleeping area is meant for one person, a single backpacking-style sleeping pad may be all you need. If there will always be two of you, a larger mattress or two backpacking-style pads will be necessary for a good night's sleep and a harmonious relationship.

I use a 3.5-inch-thick self-inflating camping pad in my SUV. It works perfectly for me. It is an air mattress that includes layers of insulating closed-cell foam, and I can make it as cushy or firm as I want. I can deflate it and roll it up in thirty seconds when I need to store it (either in the back of the SUV or in a closet at home). The pad is wider than half the width of my sleeping area, so two pads of that size wouldn't fit side-by-side without some scrunching or overlap, though I do have an additional narrow inflatable backpacking sleeping pad that fits next to my main pad if I have company.

As far as bedding goes, it can be as simple or fancy as you want. Some people like sleeping bags while others prefer sheets and blankets. I use all of these. I have a rectangular cotton sleeping bag liner that slides over the top of my air mattress and acts like a fitted sheet. On warm nights I'll use just a sheet to cover myself. On cool nights I'll use a sheet and a blanket. And on cold nights I'll use

Figure 22. Pillows and a bed in the sleeping area behind the driver's seat

a sheet, a blanket, and an unzipped sleeping bag used as a blanket. If the night is super cold, I'll get inside of the sleeping bag and layer everything else on top. If you do prefer a sleeping bag, consider using a sheet or sleeping bag liner in conjunction with the sleeping bag for two reasons: (1) you may prefer the texture and feel of a cotton sheet against your skin rather than the slick nylon or polyester liner that sleeping bags often have, and (2) it is easier to wash a sheet than a sleeping bag. If you're buying a sleeping bag specifically for camping in your SUV, pay attention to the comfort of the interior liner fabric if you don't use a separate liner. If you are in camp for the day and the weather and surroundings are appropriate, you can inject some freshness into your bedding by airing it out over the top of your SUV or by hanging it from a line strung between trees.

I have two small travel pillows in my SUV. I normally sleep without a pillow, though occasionally I will use one. Having two and stacking them on top of each other helps prop my head up when I want to sit in bed and read or watch something on my smartphone or laptop.

Privacy

Why is privacy in your SUV important? You might have your own reasons, but I know that I just don't want people to be able to see me sleeping inside my SUV if I'm in a parking lot, at a trailhead, or in a crowded campsite. I like my privacy. I feel more comfortable and cozy in my SUV when I know that no one can see me inside. If you plan on camping mainly in the woods, desert, or other sparsely populated or infrequently visited area, privacy may not be such a big issue.

My SUV has tinted windows, and these go a long way toward providing some privacy, though the tinting isn't as dark as I'd like it to be. Someone would have to actively stop and peer into my windows to see me inside, but they would definitely be able to see me. Even if I had darker tint, someone would likely be able to shine a light inside and see me. And even having darkly tinted windows wouldn't prevent people outside the vehicle from seeing me if I had a light on inside.

Although I haven't yet wanted to spend the money to get a darker tint on the windows, I have inquired at a recommended local tint shop and was told that it would cost $100 to remove the current tint and $150 to get the windows re-tinted. That seemed pretty reasonable to me and is something I'd like to get done in the future. You can also get tint kits if you'd like to tint your windows yourself and save some money. Some kits come with the tint film pre-cut specifically to fit your make and model of vehicle. Keep in mind that tint laws (which windows can be tinted, how dark the tint can be, etc.) vary from state to state in the US.

Tinting aside, my first thought for creating more privacy was to cut black poster board to fit the middle and rear windows of the SUV. These pieces did the job and were easy to make, but they weren't as rigid in the window frames as I would have liked (i.e., they sagged a bit and let a bit of light escape around the edges, which in hindsight wasn't a big deal). Then I upgraded to black foam board. These pieces fit better than the poster board inserts but were a pain to insert because they fit so tightly and a pain store because they were so large and unwieldy. Pieces of corrugated cardboard could also have worked, and the lighter cardboard color on the inside of the SUV would have been good, but I would have had to spray-paint the outside of the cardboard black.

I next considered installing curtains or drapes. I scoured the internet for in-vehicle curtain ideas that didn't involve using adhesive Velcro or any type of permanent, screwed-in fixtures, but I didn't come up with much. A lot of people use sticky-backed Velcro to secure their curtains. This would certainly be the easiest way to install curtains, but I've heard of the Velcro peeling off when the vehicle gets too hot and leaving an unpleasant, gooey residue behind. I eventually saw enough ideas through researching online that I was able to piece together a system that works well for my SUV. I ordered 20 feet (6 meters) of 1/8-inch (~3.2 millimeter) shock cord, which is like stretchy paracord. I hung this cord around the interior roofline along the sides and rear of the SUV. I secured the shock cord on the sides of the vehicle by tying it to the grab handles and coat hooks. (See Figure 23.)

My SUV doesn't have handles or hooks in the far rear, but it does have holes made for anchoring children's car seats. I used small keychain carabiners as hooks to latch onto the interior slots of these holes. (See Figure 24.)

Doing all of this created a U-shaped series of lines that stretched three-quarters of the way around the SUV. (See Figure 25.) Then I sewed (or, more accurately, kindly asked my wonderful mother to sew) curtains from black ripstop

Figure 23. How and where I anchored the shock cord in the middle of one of the sides of my SUV

nylon. (See Figure 26.) The curtains attach to the shock cord with Velcro loops. When not in use, the curtains are rolled up and secured with more Velcro loops. (See Figure 27.)

I needed an anchor still farther back in the vehicle from which I could hang the rear sections of the curtains, and for that I got binder clips and slid one side of the clip into the gap between the headliner and the rear side pillar that separates the rear window from the aft side windows. (See Figure 28.)

In all I have five pieces of fabric that act as curtains for the sides and rear of the SUV. When unfurled, the side curtains either hang straight down (easier to do but more visible from the outside) or are held up against the sides of the vehicle's windows with magnets (slightly more involved of a setup but harder to

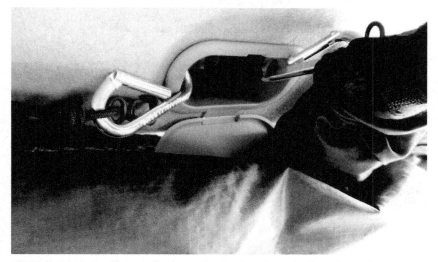

Figure 24. Small keychain carabiners used as hooks to latch shock cord onto the interior slots of children's car seat anchor holes

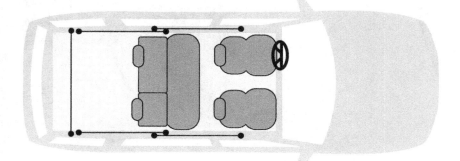

Figure 25. A top-down illustration of my SUV showing where I placed and anchored the shock cord

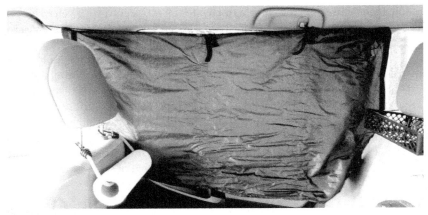

Figure 26. A side curtain deployed

Figure 27. Placement of the rolled-up curtains on the sides and rear of my SUV when seen looking back from the front

Figure 28. Using a binder clip to hold up the back end of one of the curtains. One side of the binder clip slides into the gap between the headliner and the rear side pillar that separates the rear window from the rear side windows.

detect from the outside, plus this gives me a bit more room inside the vehicle). I've also used clothespins to clip the edges of the curtains to the seatbelts that hang from the sides of the interior. This is especially useful for keeping the curtains in place when the windows are down and there's a wind. The rear curtain that covers the rear window of the vehicle hangs between the rear shelf that I have in the rear cargo area and the rear window. It can also be held in place with magnets against the metal frame of the rear window, but usually I just let it hang straight down.

The black ripstop nylon works great for my purposes of wanting more privacy. It is lightweight and takes up little space. The downside is that it is definitely not blackout fabric. When lights are on inside the vehicle, you can easily see them. This works fine for me because I do more remote camping than urban or suburban camping, and when I do camp on streets or in parking lots, I don't turn on the lights or use electronic devices when I'm in the sleeping area in the back. If you want to do something like watch movies inside of your vehicle in an urban or suburban setting, you'll need to use real blackout fabric that effectively seals up your entire vehicle. A temporary alternative to using to blackout fabric is to put a large towel, blanket, or other heavy piece of cloth over your head, shoulders, and arms to contain the light of the screen of your smart phone or tablet, though doing so would be miserable in hot weather.

Hanging these curtains gave me some privacy on the sides and rear of the vehicle, but that still left me with being visible to anyone looking in from the completely non-tinted windshield or front side windows. My first thought was to string more shock cord from the grab handle above the driver's seat to the grab handle above the front passenger's seat and then hang a black curtain from that, but I eventually came to an even simpler solution. I found an actual blackout curtain that was the perfect dimensions to cover the height and width of the inside of the SUV with a little bit extra on the sides to wrap around and overlap with the side curtains. Instead of hanging the shock cord from the grip handles and then hanging the curtain from the cord, I sewed two Velcro loops onto the top of the curtain itself about 36 inches (91 centimeters) from each other. This 36 inches is the distance between the left and right front grip handles. To hang up the curtain, I simply attach one Velcro loop to each grip handle and I'm good to go. (See Figure 29.) When not in use, this curtain gets folded up and stored under one of the rear seats.

One thing worth mentioning to hang a front curtain from is a clothes bar. This extendable bar is made to hang either from the grip handles or garment hooks in a vehicle, and the idea is that you can hang your clothes on it when it's hung from the mid or rear grip handles. The enterprising SUV RVer can hang this from the front seat grips and then hang a curtain of some sort from it.

One of the easier ways to create some privacy in your vehicle is simply to put clothes on hangers and hang them from the clothes hooks inside the vehicle. This will keep people from seeing much through the side windows. If the clothes hooks aren't in the optimal location and the hanging clothes don't

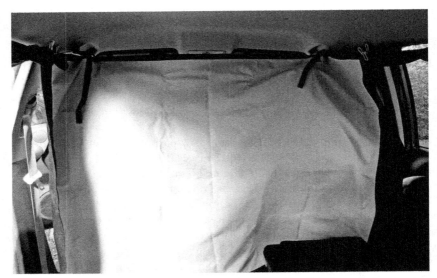

Figure 29. The front privacy curtain hanging from the grip handles above the front seats as seen from the sleeping area. The side of the curtain facing the sleeping area is white; the side facing the outside of the vehicle is black.

cover all of the window, tie some cord between the front grip handles and rear hooks and hang the clothes from this cord.

Having said and done all of this, I came to realize after actually spending many nights in my SUV that I was initially much more concerned about privacy in my SUV RV than I needed to be. It turned out that I spent much more time camping in more remote areas where the possibility of someone knowing or caring that I was sleeping in my vehicle was low. I've used my curtains a few times out of necessity but several times just for some extra coziness. They're great for blocking out the light on full moon nights. I've also found that the curtains help insulate the SUV a bit. This is great when it's cold outside but less great when the weather is hot. Indeed, the main problem with any method of window privacy (curtains, cardboard inserts, etc.) is that they either partially or entirely block air from coming into the vehicle or circulating.

You can also combine any of these methods. On a recent trip I used black poster board pieces to cover up the rear window and small porthole-style side windows and my nylon curtains to cover the main side windows. This worked very well. It was easier and faster to simply stick in and remove the poster board than unroll all of the curtains, make sure they hung down correctly, and then roll them back up again, but I liked using the side curtains because I could still easily peek out to see what was going on outside.

It's tempting when thinking about SUV RVing to overthink and overplan things before even getting out on the road. I understand this. Thinking about and planning adventures is a big part of the fun. But for all things SUV

RV-related, I recommend starting out with a minimum of equipment and then adding things one by one, as opposed to starting out with all sorts of bells and whistles and then reducing them as needed. For example, you may wish to start out with a few short one- or two-night trips as test runs without worrying about curtains or other equipment and then add more things only after you realize that you need them. After you've had some real-world SUV RVing experience, it'll be much easier to assess your needs and get the right things for a longer trip.

Temperature

Staying cool in hot weather

Few things will make your SUV RVing experience as enjoyable or miserable as the temperature inside your SUV, and the temperature inside your SUV has a lot to do with the temperature outside your SUV. If it's hot outside, it'll be hot in your SUV. If it's cold outside, it'll be cold in your SUV. It's not rocket science. "But can't I just run the heater or A/C in my SUV?" Well... You could, but (1) you'll waste gas and create unnecessary work for your engine and, more importantly, (2) you might die of carbon monoxide poisoning under the wrong circumstances. As a rule, I try not to run the engine for extended periods of time when it is stationary (though I may do it for a few minutes right before I go to sleep to get the temperature more comfortable, and I do it while sitting in the driver's seat so I'm less inclined to doze off), but I still have a carbon monoxide detector just in case when I do run it. The fear is that carbon monoxide from the tailpipe or a leak in the exhaust system will get back into the vehicle and poison you. Because you cannot smell or otherwise detect carbon monoxide without a carbon monoxide detector, always take care, especially if you are camped in a depression of some sort, are surrounded by snow banks, or are in a windless area. Many people have died from carbon monoxide poisoning in these circumstances while trying to get warm or cool in their car with the engine running.

If running the air conditioner or heater isn't an option, what can be done?

The first solution is the most obvious but still needs to be mentioned: travel when the weather is nice, and travel to places that have nice weather. This is not always feasible, but it is the best option. Sleeping in your vehicle in Texas in the middle of the summer is going to be a hot, sticky affair no matter how you look at it. Conversely, SUV RVing in Montana in January will result in less-than-optimal conditions at the other end of the temperature spectrum. Personally, I'd rather have the temperature be a bit too chilly than a bit too warm.

That leads us to the next most obvious step, and that is to dress accordingly and use the appropriate bedding materials. If it's freezing outside, bundle up and hop into your sleeping bag. If it's hot and humid, wear as little as possible and sleep under a thin cotton sheet, if anything. In general, staying warm in an SUV is easier than staying cool. You can always pile on more clothes or blankets to stay warm, but there's only so much you can take off to get cool. Sleeping on a thick, cushy foam mattress will be warmer than sleeping on a thinner foam mattress or air mattress.

If it's hot outside, there are several things you can do to make the inside of your vehicle cooler. First, you can use a fan. I have a couple of small battery-powered fans that I aim at myself, and they make a huge difference when trying to sleep on hot nights. I've also seen a much larger one that takes eight D-cell batteries. If you don't want to mess with disposable batteries, either buy rechargeable batteries, use rechargeable fans, or use USB-powered fans along with external battery packs of the type used to charge phones and tablets. To maximize air flow and circulation, take a fan, tie a loop of cord to it, and suspend it from the roof rack or an interior grab loop or clothes hook so that it hangs in front of the open window and blows air through.

A big step up from the portable fan is the roof fan. This involves cutting a square hole in the roof of your SUV, installing the fan, and hooking it up to a battery. (This is also something that you can have done for you if you don't want to do it yourself.) I know that this is a popular modification in the vandwelling community and that these fans make a huge difference by sucking out the hot, rising air. Personally, the idea of cutting a hole into the roof of my vehicle (or having someone else do it) scares me, so I haven't done this, but I see it as a great option if that isn't something that bothers you or if you have an older vehicle that you don't plan on reselling.

If your SUV has a sunroof that opens up, that could be an additional way to vent out the warm air or get a breeze, and no-see-um netting and magnets (as detailed below) could be employed to keep bugs out if they prove to be an issue. A fan placed in the sunroof to remove warm air and get airflow going would be great for hot nights and would do the work of a roof fan without the need for you to cut a hole in your vehicle's roof.

Second, assuming you are in a safe area, you can roll the windows down to get cross-ventilation going. This will help prevent condensation inside your vehicle, too. Condensation will be especially bad (and visible on windows from the outside) in cooler temperatures. You could even experiment with setting up a fan inside a side window, though this is far from stealthy and probably not the best option for urban or suburban camping. If you do roll the windows down, there's a good chance that bugs might also want to come in and bunk with you. To remedy this, I cut pieces of no-see-um netting, which has smaller holes than standard mosquito netting, and stick them over the windows of the SUV with magnets. I used to put the netting and magnets on the outside of the vehicle (Figure 30), and that worked great, but then I found an even better solution. By having the netting and magnets on the inside of the window frame (Figure 31), I can keep them there for the duration of a multi-day trip without having to set them up and take them back down again as I would if they were on the outside. When I pull into a campsite, all I have to do is roll the windows down. The only downside to this method is that it requires more magnets to get a good seal around the edges so that mosquitoes can't squeeze through.

The size of the netting is the size of the window plus a couple of extra inches on all sides. I keep these screens and magnets tucked into the pockets on the back of the front seats when not in use. There are also commercially available magnetic window screens made for specific vehicles. I haven't tried them, but I've heard good things about them.

Figure 30. No-see-um netting kept in place on the outside of the vehicle with large magnets

Figure 31. No-see-um netting attached to the inside of the vehicle's window frame by small magnets covered with duct tape

Regarding the magnets that I use to secure the bug netting, I used to use large, rectangular refrigerator magnets. These worked fine, but several of them started to fall apart; the magnets themselves became detached from the plastic housing around them. Now I use small (smaller than the diameter of my pinky finger) but powerful neodymium magnets. To make the magnets easier to handle, I wrapped them in squares of duct tape. (See Figure 32.)

Figure 32. Small but powerful neodymium magnets wrapped in squares of duct tape for easier handling. Each magnet here is smaller in diameter than a dime

Third, if possible, park your SUV so that it is perpendicular to any breeze so the breeze blows into your vehicle. Along the same lines, try not to park on the leeward side of buildings, trees, rocks, hills, or other large objects and structures that will block the wind.

The fourth way to cool your SUV is to get out of direct sunlight by parking in the shade of a tree, building, or other structure. People who camp out in hot, sunny places may want to set up sun shades, canopies, or tarps over their vehicles. (See Figure 85.)

Fifth, if you can't get out of the sun, you can try to minimize the amount of sun that gets into your SUV. One of the easiest and most common methods of doing this is to get a windshield sun shade, the kind that is reflective on the outside so that the sunlight and heat are reflected back out. The one I have folds down into a circle the size of a small dinner plate, and I keep it in the small storage compartment slot on the front driver's side door when it's not in use.

The windshield sun shade covers the front windshield, but for the other windows you can use a material called Reflectix, which is readily available by the roll at most home improvement stores or online. It's essentially thin bubble wrap with a reflective metallic layer on each side. Cut it to the appropriate size of your windows and prop it up inside the window frame (the material is stiff enough that it will stay put). This will reflect the incoming sunlight and keep it from heating the interior of your vehicle too much. The problem is that you can either open your windows to let a breeze come through or put something like Reflectix in the windows to keep the sun from coming in, but you can't do both. One option is to put Reflextix over the windows that don't roll down and keep the others uncovered. If you want to open your windows but also keep the sun from coming in, you could use an awning to provide shade, though this obviously won't work if you're in a town and trying to be discrete. (Awnings are discussed in more detail in Chapter 12, *Long-Term SUV RVing*.) A good compromise is to use Reflectix and sun shades when your SUV is parked during the day and then open the windows after the sun has gone down.

Sixth, draping a wet towel or bandana over your head, legs, feet, stomach, or chest is a super simple and effective way to cool off, especially if you also have a portable fan blowing air over you.

Finally, and I realize that this isn't something that can be easily changed, but the color of your SUV will determine how hot your vehicle gets during the day. A dark vehicle in the sun will get much hotter than a light vehicle. Keep that in mind if you're in the market for an SUV.

Keeping a small thermometer inside your vehicle is helpful if you enjoy putting a number to your level of suffering.

I've heard of vandwellers using swamp coolers to keep cool, but these don't work well in humid areas and would require a large battery bank in an SUV. If you search online for "DIY air conditioner," you'll come up with a bunch of videos, images, and articles of homemade cooling devices or evaporative coolers made from things like 5-gallon buckets, coolers, etc. I've never used one or seen one in action, so I don't know how well they work. Certainly they won't work as well as a real air conditioner, and I've heard that they are not very effective in the real world. I think that a better and simpler solution is to just use lots of fans.

If you will be staying at campgrounds that have electrical hookups or aren't averse to running a generator for hours at a time, you could get a small (~5,000 BTU) window-mounted air conditioner and set it up in one of your SUV's windows.

If your SUV is just too darn hot and stuffy, you can always sleep outside your vehicle, where you're more likely to have a breeze and good ventilation. It's a good idea to have a small tent for this purpose just in case.

Staying warm in cold weather

Staying warm when it's cold outside is much easier than staying cool when it's hot. Insulation is the name of the game here. Clothing, bedding, curtains, and other window coverings all work to insulate you. Vehicle windows are thin and uninsulated, so putting something like Reflectix in the windows will prevent warmth from escaping. In addition to being a good material to reflect the sun away from your vehicle in hot weather, Reflectix is good for keeping the warmth in. Think of it as turning your vehicle into a thermos that keeps cold liquids cold and hot liquids hot. If you want to maintain a lower profile but keep the insulation, paint one side of the Reflectix black or glue black cloth or black poster board to the side of the Reflectix that faces outward.

Because a lot of warmth is lost through the head and feet, wearing a hat (or even balaclava) and socks to bed can make a big difference. Having a thick mattress or other bedding material under you will insulate you from the cold seats, cold floor, and cold air.

Just as you should avoid parking in the sun on hot days, you should try to park in the sun on cold ones. Heating up water and pouring it into a bottle that you keep in your sleeping bag or under the covers with you is a great way to stay warm and cozy while you fall asleep. A hot drink prepared before bedtime and kept in a thermos will still be warm by morning, and that's a great way to take the edge off the morning chill.

Perhaps the worst part of SUV RVing in cold weather is the morning transition from warm covers or sleeping bag to the cold, cruel outside world. Make sure the items you need first thing in the morning are within easy reach. If you'll be changing into new clothes in the morning, consider either keeping the clothes under the covers with you or changing into them inside the sleeping bag and then waiting for them to warm up before putting them on.

Some RVers and vandwellers use small propane heaters to heat the inside of their vehicles on fierce winter nights or mornings, and this could be an option for SUV RVers. These heaters use the disposable green one-pound propane canisters. They are touted as being safe to use indoors but do require adequate ventilation to avoid carbon monoxide poisoning. The smallest portable heater I've seen can heat up a 100-square-foot room, which is definitely larger than even the largest SUV, and it burns for 5.5 hours on a single canister of propane. (Larger models can be fitted to work with the larger 20-pound propane tanks). While a propane heater would likely burn too hot for a space as small as an SUV if left on for hours, it might work well if you only need to run it for five or ten minutes to tame the harshest chill. My biggest concern is that a small propane heater like this would be a fire hazard in a space as small and confined (and full of flammable materials) as an SUV. I would personally never fall asleep with the heater running, and I would monitor it the whole time that it was on.

If you'll be camping at campsites with electrical hookups, something like an electric blanket or other type of electric heater would work well in the winter. Again, most heaters are designed to heat spaces much larger than an SUV, so you might end up with more heat (and more of a fire hazard) than you bargained for.

Rain presents an interesting conundrum for the SUV RVer, as having your windows down means that rain can get in, but having them up makes for a stifling interior during the warmer months. I've installed aftermarket deflectors on all of my windows. These are dark strips of plastic that overhang the top of the vehicle's windows by a couple of inches, making it possible to roll the windows down a few inches and not have any rain come in. These don't do much if you want to roll your windows down all the way, though. The only real option in that case would be to either park under a tree or other kind of shelter or have some sort of tarp or other covering that comes out over the windows. Some kind of down-sloping horizontal louvers that you could stick to the outside of your vehicle would work, but nothing like that exists on the market, so you'd have to make your own.

Other sleep tips

Go to the bathroom before you sleep so that you won't have to wake up in the middle of the night to do so. Try to avoid drinking fluids in the few hours leading up to bedtime. Especially avoid coffee, energy drinks, and soft drinks that contain a lot of sugar or caffeine that will keep you wired and awake.

I'm a light sleeper, and I've found that earplugs are great for letting me sleep soundly. If you want to be hyper-aware of your surroundings, however, earplugs probably aren't for you. White noise from a fan, an app, or a nearby river can also make falling asleep easier.

Sunlight and seasons need to be mentioned. Depending on where and when you are traveling, the sun may be out past your bedtime in the summer. I use a sleep mask to keep those summer or full moon nights at bay. As stated earlier, curtains are great not just for privacy but also for keeping light out.

Winter presents the opposite dilemma. I spent a few days camping near Southern California's Joshua Tree National Park in winter, and it got dark at something like 4:30 p.m. I spent the four or five hours after sundown each night reading, listening to podcasts, and watching TV show episodes that I'd downloaded to my phone. I told myself that I had to stay up till at least 8:30 p.m. before going to sleep so that I wouldn't wake up at three in the morning. If I hadn't wanted to find a campsite while it was still light outside, I could have stayed in town until later in the evening and spent my time reading or working at a café or bookstore.

I've found that I'm more active during my SUV RVing days, and that makes me more tired and ready for sleep at night, so I tend to sleep even better when SUV RVing than when in a traditional bed at home.

You'll sleep best if your SUV is parked on a flat spot and not leaning forward, backward, or to the side. I've found that sleeping at a small angle doesn't bother me, but larger ones definitely do. Pay attention to where you're parking and try to choose a spot that is level. If you find that you often need to park in places that are not level (in pull-outs off of mountain roads, for example), consider buying leveling blocks or cutting short sections of lumber that you can park on to level the vehicle out.

There is a red security light on the dashboard inside my SUV that blinks every five seconds or so, and it was bright enough that it distracted me while trying to fall asleep, so I cut out a small piece of duct tape and placed it over the light. The light is still visible but not nearly as bright as it was before. Black electrical tape would probably cover the light completely.

If your mind is at ease, you will be able to sleep better. If before bed you can take care of the things that are weighing heavily on your mind, do so. When I'm especially worked up or worried about something, I'll spend five minutes meditating before bed. This involves lying down, closing my eyes, listening to the sound of rain piped in through headphones via an app, and trying to clear my mind.

3. Storage

To see additional relevant links for this chapter, visit http://suvrving.com/book/three/.

So how exactly are you going to fit everything you want to take with you in your SUV? Before discussing the various ways to haul all of your stuff, which will be the bulk of this chapter, I want to first talk in general terms about the stuff itself.

Take less stuff

The easiest way to fit stuff into your SUV is to simply take less of it. I've spent years traveling around the world with a single carry-on bag and weeks hiking hundreds of miles with only what I could carry on my back. All of those items together could easily fit on a bicycle, let alone in an SUV, so I think it's safe to say that you will be able to fit whatever you need in your vehicle.

The question then becomes what exactly do you need in order to go SUV RVing? At the very least, you'll need two things: clothing and a bed with bedding. That's it. That's all you really need. Everything else is extra. Of course you'll probably want to take a few extra things with you, and luckily your SUV will have plenty of room for the niceties, but I wanted to highlight these necessities to emphasize the minimalist mindset you should have when SUV RVing. Chapter 4, *What to Take With You*, will cover the other things that you might want to take along.

Think about what you can "outsource." You don't need a bucket and plunger to do your laundry if you simply go to a laundromat once a week. You don't need a stove, pots, or pans if you eat out or eat foods that don't need to be cooked. You don't need a toilet if you use the facilities in stores, restaurants, and gas stations. There's no need to strap a bicycle to the top of the SUV if you don't mind renting one from time to time.

There is another angle to taking less stuff, and that is to take smaller stuff. If the things you want to take with you are small, you can fit in more items overall. For several trips I traveled with a very comfortable but very large folding camp chair. The chair itself was great, but it just took up too much space, and I had to constantly move it around the inside of my SUV to get at other stuff or do anything. Then I found a much smaller chair that could fit in just about any extra space or slot I had. It made the SUV RV life much easier because I could pack it as an afterthought instead of having to pack everything else around it. Taking small stuff applies to everything you might want to take, from shampoo bottles (think travel-sized) to lanterns (can you use a small battery-powered one instead of a massive propane one?) to games (a pack of cards instead of Trivial Pursuit and Monopoly). For washing, instead of building out a bulky and complicated sink system with plumbing and different tanks for fresh and used water, can you just use a spray bottle and plastic container?

Finally, think digitally. A smartphone alone can negate the need for things like books, maps, a compass, a camera, a flashlight, a music player, a TV, games, a GPS unit, notebooks, and an alarm clock, just to name a few. That's not to say that you shouldn't take some of those items anyway if they are important to you or if the phone versions are inferior, just that you should carefully consider everything you need before taking it with you.

I'll state again the idea that it's best to start with just the necessities and then add things from there instead of taking everything and getting rid of it later. Less is more.

Alright, now we can move on to the various storage options available to SUV RVers. In other words, where do you put all of your stuff? Some of these methods will work better for some SUVs or situations than others, and you'll likely make use of multiple methods at once. Take what will work for you and go from there.

On-seat and on-floor storage

Perhaps the easiest way to store your things is to pile them up on your seats or floors. Put stuff on the passenger seat, on the floor in front of the front passenger seat, and on the floor behind the seats. This gives you all of the rear area of your vehicle to sleep in. If only one person will be sleeping in the vehicle, half of the sleeping area can also be used for storage. Keep in mind that items stored in the sleeping area can be moved to the front seats or even the ground or roof outside when it's time to sleep.

When I'm traveling alone, I like to put my jugs of water on the floor in front of the front passenger seat. (See Figure 33.) I'll put my shoes on the floor behind the driver's seat. And my two food bins usually go on the floor behind the front passenger seat. (See Figure 34.)

Compartment storage

All vehicles have some compartments, cubbies, pockets, or slots available for storing things. The compartments in your SUV will certainly be different from the ones in mine, but below are the ones I have and what I currently use them for. Hopefully you'll get some ideas not only of what you can use these spaces for but also just how much you can fit in these spaces.

Figure 33. My cache of various water bottles and jugs and a couple of canned drinks on the floor in front of the front passenger seat

Figure 34. Shoes and food bins stored on the floor behind the front seats

Glove compartment – Here I have vehicle documents/paperwork, duct tape, clear packing tape, scissors, and a roll of toilet paper. I also sometimes put my wallet in there and lock the compartment whenever I go out for a hike or some other activity where I don't need my wallet.

Second glove compartment – Above the glove compartment is a second, smaller storage area with a sliding cover. I call it the second glove compartment. In it I put some "survival" and commonly used items, including a hairbrush, bug spray, sunscreen, a pocketknife, a headlamp, a lighter, a tape measure, tissues, binoculars, and a compass. See Figure 35 for a photo of the two glove compartments and their contents.

Below-controls slot – This is the slot below the vehicle's stereo and heat/AC controls and above the cup holders. I currently don't use it for anything except storing a Swiss Army knife because anything else tends to slide out as I drive.

Sunglasses compartment – There is a compartment in the roof near the touch lights that holds sunglasses. I use it to hold spare regular eyeglasses (I normally wear contact lenses).

Steering wheel slot – There is a very small slot left of the steering wheel that I use to hold mints and a small bottle of hand sanitizer.

Front driver's side door slot – This is a medium-sized slot that runs along the

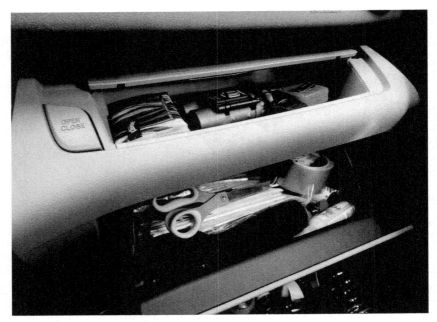

Figure 35. Items in the two glove compartments

bottom of the door. Here I have a very small pocket umbrella and my folded-up windshield sun shade. (See Figure 36.)

Front passenger door slot – In the same slot on the passenger side of the vehicle I store the brochures and maps I get from visiting national parks, museums, or other sights.

Center console slot – In this small slot in front of my center console I put a small bottle of eye drops and coins whenever I get them from a drive-thru. When convenient, I transfer the coins to the Ziploc bag inside the center console main compartment.

Center console lid compartment – The lid on my center console lifts up to reveal the main compartment inside, but the lid itself also has a small compartment. There are slots for quarters and an area for a pocket-sized notepad, a couple of pens, a permanent marker, pepper spray, and a tube of lip balm.

Center console main compartment – In the deep main compartment of the center console I have two plastic bags full of coins (one for quarters and one for all others), small bottles of vitamins and ibuprofen, a tire pressure gauge, USB charging cables, and a pair of headphones.

Driver side seatback pocket – Large bottle of hand sanitizer, bug screen with magnets, carbon monoxide detector.

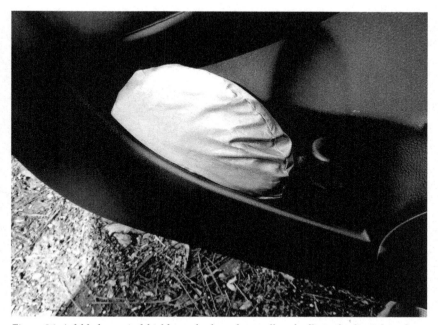

Figure 36. A folded-up windshield sun shade and a small umbrella in the front driver's side door slot

Passenger side seatback pocket – Microfiber travel towel, bug screen with magnets, drawstring bag full of plastic shopping bags that I use as trash bags.

Rear driver side door cup holder – A small spray bottle.

Rear passenger side door cup holder – Nothing. At some point I might get a wide-mouthed bottle that fits this spot and use the bottle to store small items.

Cargo area side slots and cup holders – On both the left and right sides of the rear cargo area behind the back seats is a shallow rectangular slot and a cup holder. In the slots I store the chains and locks that I use to lock down my storage bins (more on that later in Chapter 11, *Safety and Security*). In the driver side cup holder I keep earplugs and a sleep mask. In the passenger side cup holder I store a small fire extinguisher.

Side panel compartments – There are removable panels in the plastic sides of the rear cargo area. The passenger side panel holds the jack and lug wrench. The driver's side panel holds jumper cables.

Rear door net – On the rear swing-out door of my SUV is a small net pouch in which I put utilitarian objects like a small trowel, toilet paper, and tarps.

Small under-floor hidden compartment – There is a smaller hidden compartment just behind the rear seats, and that's where I store a few aerosol tire inflators (i.e., Fix-A-Flats), the towing hitch ball mount, flares, and a few other tools.

Figure 37. The rear under-floor cargo area containing items that are used less often

Large under-floor cargo compartment – The floor of my rear cargo area lifts up to reveal a somewhat hidden and relatively large storage area. This is where I put things that I won't need to access daily but that I still want to have with me. In my case, that's rock climbing gear, a sleeping bag (in the summer when a sheet and/or blanket are sufficient), some other important documents, tools, batteries, extra warm clothes, seldom-used camping gear, and my folding toilet. (See Figure 37.)

See? A lot of stuff fits into all of those compartments!

Gap storage

Your SUV probably has all sorts of nooks and crannies that are just dead space, and I make use of several of these in my vehicle.

Passenger side console gap – In the one-inch-wide (25 millimeter-wide) gap between the passenger seat and center console, I slide my US road atlas.

Driver side console gap – In this gap I store a road atlas for the states I'll be traveling through and a folder that contains printouts of information on the hikes I plan to take and the places I plan to camp at. If I don't need a road atlas, sometimes I'll also use that space to store a hanging laptop stand/holder I designed which attaches to the steering wheel. This laptop stand/holder is covered in Chapter 8, *Electronics and Internet Access*.

Rear under-seat storage – I have five or six inches of space underneath my rear seats that gets compressed down to about two inches when the seats are folded down. I've stored various things in this space, including first aid kits, portable fans, small backpacks, wet wipes, and the detachable blackout curtain that goes behind the front seats. Note that nothing should be stored under the driver's seat because you don't want anything to slide forward and possibly get in the way of the foot pedals. (See Figure 39.)

Organizers and aftermarket vehicle storage

This category of storage includes aftermarket items like seat back organizers, visor organizers, and other things made specifically for vehicle storage and organization. I currently have a couple of these. One is a visor organizer that I keep on the driver's side sun visor. It holds a pen, a permanent marker, a couple photos of my girlfriend and me, receipts, and the sunglasses that I normally drive with. I use the main zipper for receipts, and then I go through them after each trip or as necessary to tally up my expenses.

The other item in this category that I use is a visor sunglasses clip that holds two more pairs of sunglasses. Yes, I have three pairs of sunglasses: one for driving, one for hiking and rock climbing, and one for more dressy occasions.

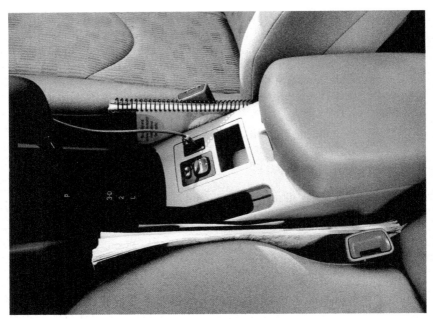

Figure 38. Road atlases and a folder stored in the gaps to the side of the center console

Figure 39. A few items stored under the rear seats

The type of organizer that contains a variety of pockets and hangs from a vehicle's headrest might also be great for SUV RVers. They can hold water bottles, toiletries, phones, tablets, and maps, among other things. Many of these can be flipped around to the front of the seat from the back and vice versa, giving different configurations for different needs.

3M's Command hooks—the hooks that can be easily installed with an adhesive strip and removed cleanly by pulling on one end of the strip—have all sorts of uses in an SUV RV. For example, I installed a clear hook onto the light that is above the middle rear seat in my SUV because I wanted a more convenient place to hang my little solar lantern. If you have any unused flat space, you could use hooks or just the adhesive strips themselves to attach storage baskets or boxes or anything that you'd like to keep handy. (See Figure 40.)

Figure 40. A small solar lantern hanging from an adhesive hook attached to the rear ceiling lights

I've seen some SUVs that have a cargo net up against the ceiling of the vehicle. If you can find one that fits your SUV, it might be a good place to store lightweight items like clothing and bedding, or you might be able to find one that is made for another purpose and repurpose it for use inside of your SUV.

Bins, boxes, and bags

Plastic bins, boxes, and drawers come in just about every shape and size imaginable and will fit whatever you need to throw in them. If necessary, you can store them in the sleeping area during the day and move them up to one of the front seats when it's time to sleep.

A plastic three-drawer chest bought from a place like Walmart can be an inexpensive and effective way to sort and store frequently used items in your vehicle. Use a bungee cord or seatbelt to keep the drawers from opening up if you find that to be a problem. In the past I've used a larger three-drawer plastic unit sitting upright on one side of the back seat (the part that I didn't have to fold down to sleep on) to hold clothes and food. I found that I didn't need to use a seatbelt or bungee cord to keep the drawers from sliding out because the angle of the bottom part of the back seat is such that the chest naturally tilted backward. I currently use a small three-drawer plastic unit on top of the rear shelf (more on the shelf below) to hold toiletries, frequently used electronics, and kitchen items. I use small plastic baskets inside each drawer to further compartmentalize and sort my things. (See Figure 41.)

Figure 41. A plastic drawer held in place with a bungee cord on top of the rear shelf. The photo was taken from the inside of the vehicle facing back.

I use plastic bins stacked on the rear passenger side seat or floor in front of the back seat to hold food. I noticed that they would slide around on the back seat while I drove, and buckling them in with the seat belt kept them in place nicely. I currently have a large black plastic bin that slides into the back of my SUV and fits perfectly. This is where a majority of my won't-use-it-daily-but-I-still-need-it stuff is kept. (See Figure 42.)

Duffel bags, backpacks, and other bags are easy storage methods that you probably already have laying around and can, depending on their contents, be stuffed and crammed into areas that aren't the right size for bins.

Hanging things

There are all sorts of places in an SUV to tie things to or hang things from. I kept losing track of the little lantern I use at night, so I ended up tying a loop of cord from one of the headrests and then using a small keychain carabiner to attach the lantern's handle to the loop of cord. Now the lantern has its own dedicated spot, and I'll never have to look for it again. (See Figure 43.)

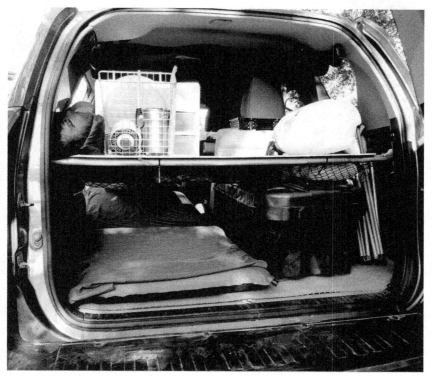

Figure 42. A look at the rear setup of my SUV in sleeping mode. The sleeping area is on the left, and the large black storage bin is on the right. The shelf above gives even more surface area for storage.

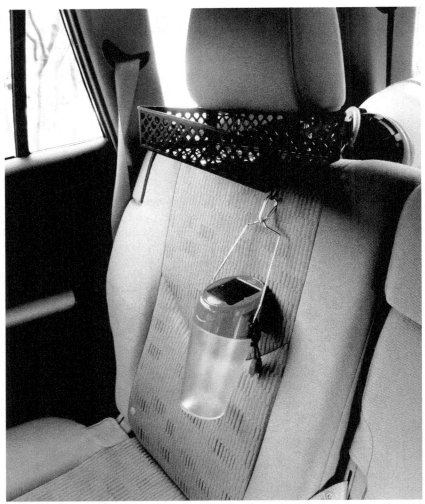

Figure 43. The small basket that I place my keys, phone, wallet, and other items in before bed. The lantern hangs from a piece of cord below it.

One thing I missed in my SUV was a bedside table. I wanted a place where I could put things like my phone, wallet, keys, and other little items that I keep in my pockets. I tried a few different setups, but the one I like best is also the simplest. I took a little plastic basket and tied it to the headrest posts above where I store the lantern. It's perfect! And after taking a good look at my storage solutions during an extended trip, I realized that I had unused storage space in the form of the headrest itself. It became the ideal place to store the fanny pack I use for hiking (I shortened the straps and buckled it around the headrest) and my sun hat (I plopped it over the top of the headrest).

Under-platform storage

One of the main benefits of having a platform-style sleep system—the "table" that you can sleep on—in your SUV is that it creates room underneath for gear (though at the cost of headroom height between the surface of the platform and the ceiling of your vehicle). Depending on your SUV and the platform you build, you may be able to access the space underneath the platform either from the rear door of the vehicle and/or the side doors. If there are areas under the platform that can't easily be reached these ways, you can create hatches or panels in the surface of the platform that you can lift up to give you better access.

Bins can usually slide under the platform, and smaller bins, bags, or individual items can be placed in the irregular spaces between the larger bins.

The rear shelf

The rear shelf is, in my opinion, an essential storage system in the SUV RV, assuming it makes sense in your vehicle's layout, and it adds a significant amount of cargo capacity. It consists of a single flat rectangle a couple of feet (60 centimeters) or so in depth that spans the width of the rear cargo area. The idea is that you can store gear under the shelf during the day while driving and then put the gear on top of the shelf at night when it's time to sleep (your feet go under the shelf where the bins were stored during the day). (See Figure 44.)

Figure 44. The rear shelf in action. The bin on top of the shelf is stored below the shelf when the SUV is in motion but placed on top of the shelf when it's time to stretch out for the night. The bin on the floor of the cargo area could be placed on top of the shelf to create room for a second sleeper. Note the white PVC pipe support legs.

The surface of the shelf can be a piece of wood, a metal rack, a few lengths of pipe, or a few pieces of 2x4 wood. Depending on the size of what you need to put on top of the shelf, it's not a problem if there are gaps in the surface of the shelf. (See Figure 45.)

Assuming you don't want to screw the shelf into the sides of your SUV, you'll need some way to support it. As with the sleeping platform, this can be done with pieces of wood or pipe. The easiest shelf system to build would just be a piece of plywood for the top surface of the shelf with a supporting leg of wood in each corner, and the shelf system would sit squarely on the floor of the SUV. But the back cargo areas of most SUVs often have storage compartments, wheel wells, or other non-level areas or inconsistencies to deal with, and it's possible that the two fore legs will have to be at different lengths than the two rear ones.

Depending on how heavy the items that you'll be putting on top of the shelf are, you might have to add additional support pieces underneath the shelf.

Another way to create the shelf legs is to use PVC pipe or copper tubing to create the form and legs and then put a piece of wood on top that can be secured to the frame with pipe brackets, U-bolts, or cable ties. Or the entire thing including the top surface of the shelf could even be made out of pipe or pieces of wood.

One important thing to keep in mind regarding the shelf is that it needs to be at a height where your storage bins or bags will fit both underneath it and on top of it. And of course you'll want the shelf high enough off the floor of the cargo area that when you are in bed, your feet can fit there without accidentally kicking the shelf when you move around during the night.

My SUV actually has holes on the sides of the rear cargo area, and it took me a while before I realized that those holes were actually for an aftermarket shelf that consists of two aluminum bars (the ends of which slide into the holes) and a net between the bars to hold smaller objects. It is marketed as a net but works great as a shelf for my bins. (See Figure 46.)

Figure 45. A diagram of a simple shelf that could be made from pipe or wood. Note the difference in length between the rear and front legs to account for the wheel well.

Figure 46. The bare aftermarket shelf/net setup that I use

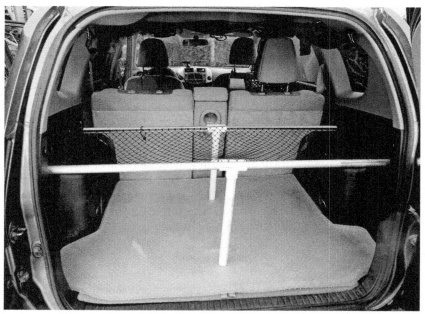

Figure 47. The aftermarket shelf/net setup with easily removable PVC support legs for heavier loads

This shelf/net was made specifically for my SUV (a Toyota RAV4), but I mention it here for you to look around to see if there is something like that for your vehicle. The downside is that it isn't made to hold the weight of bins full of equipment, so I cut some PVC legs and 3-way tee fittings to act as supports. I cut out a chunk of PVC on the top of each tee fitting to make the support legs nonpermanent and easily removable. (See Figure 47.)

After several trips using this setup, I decided to take a thin piece of wood and add it over the top of the bars to act as a more rigid platform for whatever I wanted to put on top. I attached the thin plywood platform to the tubing of the shelf using just two cable ties on one side. Now I can actually lift up the shelf as if it were on a hinge and still put stuff underneath it. I essentially doubled the storage capacity of the shelf. It's the perfect place to store my clothes. (See Figure 48.)

Before buying the shelf/net that was made specifically for my model of vehicle, I actually cut three lengths of 1-inch diameter PVC pipe to the width of the interior of my SUV and slotted those into the holes to form a shelf. This worked surprisingly well, but I ended up buying the shelf/net because it was much easier and faster to put in and take out, which I thought I might want to do occasionally (though it hasn't been the case; I haven't removed the shelf since putting it in it).

Built-ins

If you really want to customize the interior of your SUV, you can build cabinets, cubbies, tables, or storage areas specifically for your vehicle. These things can be permanently attached to your SUV or simply placed on top of the floor and/or seats.

The good things about built-ins in an SUV are that they can be customized to your exact specification and that they can give the SUV a more homey "this is my own space" kind of feel, which could be nice on a long trip. The big downside to built-ins is that they are not very flexible once installed. Once they're in, they're hard to customize further if you find that your needs or wants change later on. On top of that, you'll have to store them somewhere when you're not using them between trips. If you do want to go the built-in route, I'd recommend starting out with one of the easily removable storage options (bins, boxes, bags, etc.) and then upgrading later on once you've got your systems all ironed out and figured out exactly what you want in a setup.

The roof

The roof of an SUV is an obvious place to store items. It gets stuff out of the way so that you can have a much more open and uncluttered interior. Or if you don't mind the cluttered interior, storing things on the roof means that you can haul around even more stuff with you.

Figure 48. The surface of the shelf lifted to reveal extra storage for clothing or other items on the net below

There are a few different ways to store items like bins, boxes, bags, suitcases, strollers, etc. on the roof of your vehicle. The first is to simply strap them to the roof using ratchet straps or tie them down with rope. While this can work, it can also be dangerous if the items are not tied or anchored correctly, and it is difficult to quickly and easily access your stuff. Still, if you're on a budget and have good tie-downs, this option can work. Having a roof rack will make tying things down easier and more secure, and a rooftop cargo basket is an even better option if you will routinely be using the roof for storage. (See Figure 49.)

The second way to use the roof is to get a rooftop bag. These are large, soft-sided, often weatherproof bags made specifically to fit on top of a vehicle. The bag can be attached to the vehicle's roof rack or, if there is no roof rack, by straps that pass through the side doors of the vehicle and essentially hug the roof. (See Figure 50.)

You can also buy padded roof mats to put under your rooftop items or bag. A mat provides extra padding that protects the top of your vehicle from scratches and extra grip that helps keep the items or bag in place.

The biggest downside to these rooftop storage options is that your items are not completely safe and secure. It would be relatively easy for someone to steal them from off the top of your vehicle because any straps used to hold items down could be cut and the rooftop bags sliced open. Another negative is that there is a greater chance that anything stored on the roof could get wet

Figure 49. A rooftop cargo basket attached to a roof rack

Figure 50. A rooftop bag strapped to the roof rack

when exposed to the elements. But for items that are bulky, replaceable, or not terribly valuable—or if you'll be in remote places and are unconcerned about things potentially being stolen from your vehicle—these "soft" rooftop storage options are worth a look.

The third way to use your roof for storage is to use specialized racks or rack fittings for things like bicycles, skis, canoes, kayaks, surfboards, or gas cans. These racks or fittings may be able to lock, depending on the kind you get.

The fourth way to use your roof for storage is to get a cargo box, also known as a car top carrier. These are hard-sided plastic or composite bins that attach to a roof rack. The big benefit with these is that they are generally waterproof, lockable, and able to swallow a ton of gear (depending on the size you get, of course). These range in price from a couple hundred dollars up to more than a thousand dollars. (Look on classifieds websites to find good deals on used ones;

often people will buy one of these for a single trip and then just want to get rid of it afterward.) If there will be more than one person in your SUV, if you don't want to deal with lots of stuff and clutter inside your vehicle, or if you simply have more things to carry than room to carry them, the rooftop cargo box is the way to go.

There are some downsides to cargo boxes. First, they're enormous and take up a lot of space when not being used on top of your vehicle. In other words, you'll have to store the thing if you ever want to take it off. Second, they can negatively impact the fuel efficiency of your vehicle. Depending on the vehicle and box, the difference can be as little as one or two miles per gallon or as high as 35% of overall efficiency. Third, again depending on the one you have, it can create unpleasant wind noise when driving at high speeds. Finally, the added height to the top of your SUV means that you may not be able to drive through certain fast food restaurants or fit into some parking garages. I remember going on a family road trip as a kid when we had a large cargo box on top of our minivan. Our dad offered to give any of us kids five dollars if we reminded him about the cargo box before accidentally going through a drive through. Sure enough, somewhere along the way, we were about to drive through a McDonald's when my sister reminded our dad about the big thing on the roof. A crisis was averted, and my sister was five dollars richer.

There's one more thing to consider when buying a cargo box, and that is the way that it opens. Some open from the rear and others open from the side. If your SUV doesn't have a place for you to stand on the rear bumper, a side-opening cargo box might make more sense unless you can stand on top of a footstool, chair, bin, or something else.

One thing that needs to be said about all rooftop storage options—and all external storage options in general—is that they can draw too much attention to your vehicle if you want to be unobtrusively sleeping inside.

The front

It's rare to store things on the front of an SUV. A winch is one thing you often see here, and I've seen photos of bicycle racks that attach to the front of the vehicle, but that's about it.

The back

Rounding out the exterior storage options for an SUV is the back of the vehicle. Each SUV model is unique. Some rear doors open upward, while others swing out to the side. Some SUVs have spare tires on the back, while others don't. Not each of the options listed below will work on every vehicle.

Trailer hitches (or, more specifically, trailer hitch receivers) are relatively inexpensive and easy to install if you don't already have one on your SUV, and they open up a number of storage options at the rear of the vehicle. The first is what is usually referred to as a hitch cargo carrier, and it's essentially a platform or basket that attaches to a square hitch. (See Figure 51.) This is a great and cost-effective way to carry bulky things like a cooler, a generator, large water jugs, or plastic bins. The only problem with these is that the height of the objects on them can prevent you from opening the rear door of the SUV. Some hitch cargo carriers solve this by being on a swing arm that can swing off to the side and out of the way of the door, but these types of carriers are much more expensive than the ones that are stationary. Another variation is similar to the flat or basket-like hitch cargo carrier but is a big, heavy-duty bin instead of just the platform. These lock and are therefore more secure than simply placing items on a flat shelf or in a basket.

Another rear storage solution is the hitch-mounted bike rack. It is similar to the hitch cargo carrier but designed specifically for bicycles, and it has the benefit over roof-mounted bicycle racks of not increasing the overall height of the vehicle. You can continue making those late-night fast food drive-thru runs without the worry of extra height on your vehicle. Most of these bike racks share the same drawback of many hitch cargo carriers in that they can make it difficult or impossible to open the rear door. But as with the hitch cargo carriers, there are some hitch-mounted bike racks that swivel out or come forward and down to give you access to the vehicle's cargo area.

Spare tire hitch mounts exist and may be a good option for people who do a lot of backcountry exploration in their SUVs. And speaking of spare tires, the spare comes standard on the back some SUVs like Jeeps and pre-2013 Toyota RAV4s, and owners of vehicles like this can buy brackets that attach to the tire that will hold gas cans or other items.

Trailers

If you want to haul a lot of stuff with your SUV, you can always get a trailer for it. A camper trailer could be used to sleep in while you store stuff in your SUV, or you could get a cargo trailer and sleep in the SUV while storing stuff in the trailer. The added length of a trailer would, of course, dramatically affect the number of places that you could access and camp at.

Figure 51. A hitch-mounted cargo carrier

Organization and clutter

Here are some brief general guidelines for dealing with your stuff that will make your SUV RVing experience better:

1. Be organized. Have a place for everything so that you know how to find it and can easily put it back after use.

2. The less stuff you have, the better. It will make cleaning easier and will make your SUV a more pleasant space to be.

3. Try to take smaller versions of the items you do decide are worth taking.

4. Use things that have multiple purposes. For example, instead of taking a big plastic bin and a camp table, use the plastic bin as a camp table.

5. Buy the right thing. If there's something you really need or want, save up and buy that instead of a cheaper alternative. In a small space like an SUV, it's great to be surrounded by stuff you really love.

6. Try to limit taking things "just in case" unless they could potentially be life-saving.

4. What to Take With You

To see additional relevant links for this chapter, visit http://suvrving.com/book/four/.

This chapter covers a bunch of things that you'll want to consider taking with you as you explore in your SUV RV. Not all of these will make sense for every trip. Think of this chapter as a packing list that you can pick and choose from to suit your needs. This list is based on what I have traveled with in the past, what I currently travel with, and what I may choose to travel with in the future, and your needs and wants will undoubtedly be different from mine.

Clothing

Clothes are a necessity for any trip (unless you frequent nudist resorts), and a trip in an SUV is no exception. The exact clothing you'll need will depend heavily on where you plan to go and the time of year you plan to go there.

In my normal day-to-day life, I usually wear jeans and a t-shirt, so that's what I pack when I travel in my SUV. As a general rule, I pack clean underwear, socks, and shirts for each day of the trip, and one pair of pants for every few days. If my trip will last longer than a week, I pack a week's worth of clothing and do laundry at a laundromat once a week. When cool or cold places are on the itinerary, I add to my packing list a couple of long-sleeve shirts, a waterproof/breathable jacket, a fleece jacket, a down jacket, and a warm hat.

The material of your clothing is something you should pay attention to. Most of my normal clothing is cotton. It's cheap, cool, and comfortable. But I hike a lot, and it's not the best for hiking because it retains moisture and does not insulate when wet. So in addition to my normal clothing, I pack hiking-specific clothing. Some of this is made from merino wool. Though expensive, this material is light, breathable, and resistant to odor, so it's great for socks, underwear, and t-shirts. There are stories of people wearing the same merino wool shirt for weeks at a time while traveling and not smelling too terrible afterward. I wore the same merino wool t-shirt everyday for thirteen days when I hiked the 220-mile-long John Muir Trail in California's Sierra Nevada mountains. I won't say that I emerged from the wilderness smelling like roses, but I was amazed by how much the shirt didn't smell. In addition to merino wool, I also have hiking

Figure 52. Slacks and a dress shirt hanging from a garment hook inside an SUV

clothing made from nylon or polyester. This material is tough, and it wicks moisture (i.e., sweat) away from the body. I've found that it does get smellier than the natural fabrics like cotton or wool, but it dries faster than cotton and is much cheaper than wool.

Because I'm often hiking during the day, it's nice to change into clean clothes at night. I like to use one set of clothing as camp clothing, and I change into it after a sweaty day of hiking.

I fold most of my clothes and used to store them either in a bin or bag. Some people find that rolling their clothes works better. As mentioned earlier, I now keep my clothes suspended in the netting below the rear shelf. I put dirty clothes in a bag and store the bag inside my large plastic storage bin so they don't stink up the place. On a longer trip, I keep a nicer pair of slacks and a dress shirt hanging up on hangers from the back seat garment hook. (See Figure 52.) The downside of hanging clothes by a window if you've parked at a popular camping area and have the windows rolled down is that your clothes may end up smelling like other people's campfire smoke.

Navigation

While there is a certain charm in getting lost if there is no danger or time restraint, I usually like to get where I'm going without taking unnecessary detours. Below are the items I use for that.

Smartphone – I use my smartphone as a GPS unit. It works great 95% of the time. I have a suction cup dashboard mount that I place the phone in while I'm driving. The 5% of the time that it doesn't work is when I'm out of cellular range and can't download new maps. Earlier this year I spent several days without cellular coverage as I drove from small town to small town in southern Utah, and I had to find restaurants with WiFi service in order to download new maps to figure out where I was going. I would have loved to have a stand-alone GPS unit with all maps pre-loaded onto it, and I will likely be getting one in the future for this kind of situation. Some mapping apps for smartphones will let you download maps to use offline, and it's a good idea to do that if you know your trip will take you to far-out places.

Country road atlas – I keep a nationwide US road atlas in the vehicle at all times. It is great for getting a bird's-eye view of an area and for planning the broad strokes of a road trip. The particular atlas I have shows major points of interest and has introduced me to all sorts of great sights I otherwise wouldn't have known about, from a jelly bean factory to deserted sand dunes to World War II internment camps. I also use this atlas to plan where I'm going to camp, as it has national forests marked. (More details on this are in Chapter 5, *Where to Camp*.)

State road atlas – If I'll be spending a lot of time in one particular state, I'll buy a detailed state road atlas. Everything about these state atlases is more detailed, from city maps to backroads to state and national parks to points of interest. A good state atlas will also show much more topographic detail and will show national forests, BLM (Bureau of Land Management) land, etc. These atlases are especially useful for those SUV RVers who like to explore in more depth and get off the beaten path.

Printouts – Before going on a trip, I will print out information about potential campsites or hikes and the details on how to get to the campsites or trailheads. I put these printouts into a folder that I slide into the gap between the center console and the front passenger seat.

Sleeping

Items needed for sleeping were covered in Chapter 2, but I'll again list the essential items here:

- Mattress(es) or sleeping pad(s) – You may need more than one if there will be more than one of you sleeping inside the vehicle.
- Bedding (e.g., sheets, sleeping bag, etc.)
- Pillow(s)
- Sleep mask and earplugs
- Curtains or other window covering

- Bug netting and magnets for the windows
- Battery-powered fans

Electronics

These and more of the electronics that you may want to take are covered in depth in Chapter 8, *Electronics and Internet Access*, but here is a good list of starting items for most people:

- Inverter – An inverter lets you plug in and charge your electronic devices from your vehicle's battery. I recommend one with both 120-volt wall-type outlets and USB ports.
- Smartphone with dash mount
- Tablet and/or e-reader
- WiFi hotspot
- Charging cables
- Spare batteries
- Digital camera with case, memory card, spare batteries, and charging cable
- External battery packs
- Small solar panel
- Laptop with whatever peripherals you need or want (mouse, speakers, etc.)

Vehicle stuff

- Fix-A-Flat cans
- Digital tire pressure gauge
- Vehicle registration and other documentation
- Spare tire
- Jack
- Tire iron
- Air compressor
- Jumper cables
- Emergency jumper battery unit
- Extra fuel

Camping gear

- Camp table
- Camp chair(s)
- Headlamp
- Lantern – Mine can be charged via either USB or the little solar panel on top of it. When I park my vehicle on a sunny day, I'll try to position the vehicle so that the sun is coming in through the front windshield, and then I'll prop the lantern up on top of the dashboard so it can charge.

- Backpack
- Axe or hatchet
- Folding shovel
- Tarp
- Rope/cord
- Tent stakes

Tools, etc.

- Duct tape
- Packing tape
- Scissors
- Pens, pencils, and permanent markers
- Hammer
- Screwdrivers
- Pliers and needle-nosed pliers
- Cordless drill/screwdriver
- Saw
- Wrenches

Toiletries, etc.

- Tissues
- Paper towels
- Toothbrush and toothpaste
- Floss
- Hand sanitizer
- Travel towel
- Wet wipes
- Spray bottle
- Travel shower
- Deodorant
- Glasses
- Contact lenses
- Camp toilet
- Small mirror
- Sunscreen
- Bug spray
- Soap
- Shampoo

Cooking, etc.

- Stove
- Stove fuel canisters

- Lighter/matches
- Can opener
- Bottle opener
- Pot with lid
- Frying pan
- Hot pad
- Plates, bowls, cups/mugs
- Eating utensils
- Cooking utensils (e.g., large spoon, spatula, etc.)
- Knives
- Salt and pepper
- Other spices
- Bins, coolers, and/or a refrigerator for food
- Water bottles

Emergencies/Safety

- Lighter/matches
- Small fire extinguisher
- Flares
- Poncho
- Space blanket/emergency blanket
- Carbon monoxide detector
- Smoke detector
- Compass
- First aid kit
- Maps

Other stuff

- Binoculars
- Quarters – When you're not traveling, save and stockpile your quarters for future trips. You'll be able to use them on the road for things like doing laundry and washing the vehicle, not to mention getting a Coke from a vending machine every now and then and paying tolls.
- Trash bags
- Vitamins
- Vehicle documents
- Mints

Final words on packing

There are three parts to figuring out what the perfect packing list is for you. First, do your research and think about what you'll need. Second, take that stuff and go on a trip. Third, take a look at all of your stuff when you get back home and see what you used and what you didn't. There will be some things like a fire extinguisher that you probably didn't use but that you should take on your next adventure anyway. But there will also be things that you thought would be useful but weren't, or that didn't work the way you wanted them to. Repeat this post-trip scrutinizing after every trip and you'll eventually have a fine-tuned setup that is absolutely perfect for your needs and wants.

5. Where to Camp

To see additional relevant links for this chapter, visit http://suvrving.com/book/five/.

One of the greatest things about SUV RVing is the ability to sleep pretty much anywhere, and learning to figure out the best places to spend the night is one of the most important arrows to have in your SUV RVing quiver. This chapter aims to be a big part of that education. Where you sleep can mean the difference between waking up in the morning feeling refreshed and waking up in the middle of the night because a police officer is giving you a ticket for parking illegally. If it's hot out and you were sleeping in your underwear (not recommended in urban or suburban camping), that's going to be a very awkward encounter.

Something that needs to be mentioned before digging into the details of where to camp is that winter can make things more difficult. Many campgrounds close in the winter. Many roads (dirt roads in particular) at high elevations are either officially closed in the winter or practically impassable due to snow levels. Even on roads that are plowed, there may be pullouts (in which you could potentially park and spend the night under normal conditions) that are unplowed and full of snow. Streets in urban or suburban areas can have piles of snow on the sides of the road that the plows have pushed aside, making street parking difficult or impossible. Just be aware that depending on where you are, winter can provide significant camping challenges.

BLM land

BLM stands for Bureau of Land Management. It is a government organization that oversees and manages the use of public lands in the United States. This includes 264 million acres of land, mostly in the western US. If all of those millions of acres of land were lumped together into one contiguous body, the resulting land mass would be smaller than Alaska but larger than Texas. It's a lot of land.

The BLM states on its website (*http://blm.gov*) that its mission "is to manage and conserve the public lands for the use and enjoyment of present and future generations under our mandate of multiple-use and sustained yield." In

...lands are generally open to the public for everything from shooting, riding a dirtbike to camping in a tent to, yes, parking and sleeping in an RV. With the right permits and permissions, this land can also be used by individuals and corporations for grazing cattle, hunting, logging, gathering firewood, and drilling for oil. The BLM hands out these permits.

In most, if not all, BLM land areas, there is a 14-day camping limit. More specifically, the rule states:

"A person may not occupy undeveloped public lands or designated sites or areas for more than 14 days within a 28 consecutive day period. Following the 14 days, a person and their personal property must relocate to a site outside of at least a 25-mile radius from the occupied site for a period of 14 days."[2]

In other words, you can stay in one spot for up to 14 days in a 28-day period but then you must move at least 25 miles away for another 14 days before you can go back. I can't see this as being an issue for the vast majority of SUV RVers, as 14 days in one spot is a substantial chunk of time. I've heard some long-term campers say that in practice, all they have been told to do by patrolling rangers is move their rig twenty feet to the right and that's good enough. In other areas, the 14-day rule is strictly enforced. Some very popular BLM open camping areas may have a camp host that you need to check in with before camping.

You also need to know that certain smaller areas within BLM land may have different regulations. Some wilderness areas, for example, may require permits for overnight use. And while most BLM land is fee-free for general use, certain places—picnic areas with bathrooms or parking at very popular trailheads, for example—may require a fee.

Otherwise, you can just find a nice, quiet spot on BLM land and park there for the night, and you have most of that bigger-than-Texas land to choose from. This 100% free and legal camping is called dispersed camping. You won't find water, toilets, showers, and picnic tables here; instead, it's just you and your SUV out in the middle of nowhere. (See Figure 53.) There are established campgrounds on BLM land (more on this later in the chapter), but you'll have to pay for them. If you want to use a toilet, you'll often find them on BLM land at popular trailheads, archaeological sites, natural attractions, viewpoints, and other points of interest.

All of this sounds great, right? So how can you actually find out where BLM land is? First, if you just want a quick overview of land ownership in a particular state, simply do an online image search for "public lands in Idaho map" or similar for whatever state you're interested in. Look for a map that includes BLM lands.

The second method is to visit the BLM online (*http://blm.gov*) and try to navigate their outdated website to find the state you're looking to recreate in and then try to find maps of certain areas within that state. This is really the best option only if you have a specific piece of BLM land in mind (that you also know the name of) that you would like a map for. And even then, it might be

Figure 53. Free dispersed camping on BLM land near Lake Havasu City, Arizona

easier to just search online for the specific map you want.

The third and easiest way to find BLM land is to go to find a website that shows public lands as overlays on top of regular maps. For this I use the Public Lands Interpretive Association's website (*http://publiclands.org*), though there may be better options by the time you read this. Go there and select the state you're interested in. A map of that state will then pop up, and under the "Public Lands" header on the left side of the map, you can tick the box next to "Bureau of Land Management Lands" to see an overlay map. (If you've clicked the box and don't see any changes, make sure the "Land Status" box in the bottom-right corner of the map is checked.)

A similar online mapping tool is called GeoCommunicator (*http://www.geocommunicator.gov/blmMap/Map.jsp?MAP=LAND*). I personally find the publiclands.org maps easier to use, but your mileage may vary.

The fourth option is to use a mobile app. This puts the above-mentioned map overlay data onto your phone. Because apps come and go, I won't recommend a specific app here in the book. To find an app that works for you, search for "US public lands" in the app store of your choice and take a look at the options that come up.

While nice paved roads do cut through BLM lands, to find good campsites there's a good chance you'll have to drive at least a short distance on dirt roads. Any SUV that hasn't been turned into a low-rider should be able to handle this without a problem, though there will be other roads that are too rough for all but the most beefed-up rigs (or ambitious/foolhardy drivers).

What do you do after you've found a chunk of BLM land to camp on? If I'm planning ahead, I'll look on a map for prominent dirt roads that lead through the area. Then I'll switch to the satellite view of the area on a computer or phone and look for large pullouts along the side of the road or spur roads leading off from that dirt road that end in what looks like a dirt cul-de-sac. It's these large pullouts and dirt cul-de-sacs that I'll pull into for the night. The odds are good that I won't be the first person to have camped there, and it's common for me to find existing fire rings and other indicators of previous overnight usage at these sites.

If I'm not planning ahead, I'll still do what I mentioned above. I'll drive through the BLM land and look for side roads that lead off into potential camping areas, side roads that have wide pullouts, or short spur side roads that dead-end quickly. These are all potential camping areas.

The Long-Term Visitors Areas on BLM land in the desert of southeastern California and southwestern Arizona are another option for SUV RVers. As the BLM states on its website, these "are specially designated areas ... [that] provide places for visitors to stay for longer periods of time between September and April. A seasonal special recreation permit [$180] is required, and the permit allows visitors to stay in any of the six LTVAs in California or two LTVAs in Arizona" [*http://www.blm.gov/ca/st/en/fo/elcentro/recreation/ltvas.html*]. Having one of these permits means that you can legally stay in one the spot at an LTVA for months at a time, and some of the areas even have trash services, dump stations, restrooms, and water sources.

National forests

National forests are forests that are under the stewardship of the US government (specifically the Forest Service) to do with as it sees fit. Practically speaking, it's easiest for SUV RVers to think of national forests as BLM land with trees. They offer the same advantages as BLM land in that you can pretty much park your SUV anywhere and camp. (See Figure 54.)

A great thing about national forests is that a good national road atlas will have them marked as beautiful rectangular bodies of green and labeled as national forests, unlike BLM land, which is usually only marked in state atlases. When you see these areas on the map, you know that there are free campsites to be had.

Dispersed camping is allowed in most national forest areas unless otherwise noted. Once you find on a map a national forest that you'd like to camp in, go find the website for that national forest (it'll be a sub-page of the US Forest Service website at *http://fs.usda.gov*) and look at the section about camping. These pages will tell you all of the rules you need to know regarding camping in these areas. The pages may also suggest dispersed camping areas in addition to the established campgrounds.

Figure 54. Free camping in Gifford Pinchot National Forest just outside of Washington's Mt. Rainier National Park

My tactics for finding a place to sleep in a national forest are very similar to my tactics for finding a place to camp on BLM land. Usually I'll be driving on a nice paved road through the national forest and looking for dirt roads that branch off into the forest from there. Many of these are current or former logging roads.

As with dispersed camping on BLM land, dispersed camping in national forests means that you won't have water, toilets, showers, and picnic tables where you camp, though again, as with BLM land, you may find toilets and picnic tables at trailheads or scenic spots like rivers and waterfalls.

Many of the national parks in the western US are surrounded by forest service land, meaning that instead of paying for an expensive and crowded campground at a national park, you can instead camp for free by yourself in the neighboring national forest.

Because national forests are broken into distinct chunks and given distinct names, it's easy to search for more information about them. For example, before hiking in Washington's Mt. Rainier National Park, I saw that much of the park was surrounded by Gifford Pinchot National Forest. I checked online to make sure there weren't any specific restrictions for camping in the national forest (there weren't that I didn't already know) and was good to go. I spent a couple of nights there just minutes from the entrance to the national park and was completely alone.

Other public lands

Other public lands under government care include national parks, national monuments, national wildlife refuges, national recreation areas, national conservation areas, and national and state recreation areas. The rules for camping in each of these areas are different, but more information about them can easily be found by searching for them by name online. I mention them here because they are places that, if you see them on a map, can be potential places to spend the night.

The only one of the above-mentioned places that I'll go into more detail about is national parks. These are the most spectacular of our public lands and, as such, are some of the most heavily guarded and protected. Generally speaking, camping is not permitted in these parks outside of designated campsites and campgrounds.

Most national parks, many national monuments, and some other public lands, including certain BLM and national forest areas, require entrance fees. An annual pass is essential for SUV RVers who plan to visit a lot of these sites. At the time of this writing, an annual pass costs $80 for a year's worth of unlimited entrance access to national parks, national monuments, BLM lands, and national forests that require an entrance fee. It doesn't work for state or other locally administered parks, but because a one-time fee for a single vehicle to enter a national park can be as much as $30, it makes a lot of financial sense to get the annual pass if you plan to visit the national lands often.

Public campgrounds

Public campgrounds are campgrounds operated on public lands. These are often found in national parks, national monuments, national forests, BLM lands, state parks, and county parks. Public campgrounds are rarely free (someone's got to pay for the upkeep and maintenance of the facilities, right?), and the cost can range from $5 a night in a simple BLM campground that has flat tent sites and pit toilets to $40 for large sites with full hookups for RVs. Campsites in the national parks and other popular areas can be reserved many months in advance during the peak seasons (though there are some walk-in, first-come, first-served campgrounds in some national parks), so it's important to plan far ahead if you plan to stay in those campgrounds.

SUV RVers fall into an unusual category of camper. We don't sleep in tents, so we don't really need tent sites, but we also don't need all of the hookups that RV sites offer. I personally try to go for the tent sites. Most of the time there is a parking spot right next to the campsite, and SUV RVers can simply park and sleep there, hopefully without any problems. (You can go online to view maps of popular campgrounds to determine whether this is the case.) I have, however, seen signs in the tent camping sections of campgrounds that very clearly and explicitly state that people are not allowed to sleep in their vehicles in the tent camping parking spots. (I'm looking at you, Pine Springs Campground in West Texas's Guadalupe Mountains National Park.) I know that some people set up tents there and either sleep in the tents or still just sleep in their vehicles. Either way, it's good to have a tent in your vehicle for situations like this. The Australian girls that I camped next to at Pine Springs Campground didn't even bother with that; they just pulled up in their van and had no intentions of setting up a tent. When the campground host came by an hour later, he told them that they had to move on to the less picturesque vehicle parking area (read: parking lot), though ultimately they were able to talk their way out of it.

I've personally never slept in my SUV in an RV-specific spot, though it may be required in the campsites you visit. These campsites are usually, though not always, more expensive than the tent sites. One big benefit to staying in an RV-specific site is that you can plug in whatever electronics you have there at the campsite. This opens up a wide variety of electronic devices that might otherwise not be feasible to power, namely electric heaters, air conditioners, electric grills, and the like.

The benefits of staying in a public campground regardless of the type of campsite are as follows:

1. They're usually pretty easy to find on maps or online, so you can have a specific place to spend the night lined up in advance.

2. They are usually located in areas that even passenger cars can access, so you won't have to drive for miles on washboard roads.

3. They have facilities useful for SUV RVers. Toilets and picnic tables are obvious ones. Running water in bathrooms and at spigots throughout the campground mean that you can top up your water supply if you're running low (though check to make sure the water is potable first; also be sure to taste the water before filling up with it, because sometimes it's way too chlorinated). An ample water supply also means a potential place to hand wash laundry if desired. And perhaps most importantly, showers at these campgrounds are a godsend for those SUV RVers who prefer feeling like civilized human beings to wild creatures.

Private campgrounds and RV parks

Private campgrounds and RV parks are similar in most ways to public campgrounds, the main difference being that they are, of course, on private—not public—lands. In other words, a person or company owns these campgrounds. KOA Campgrounds are the most widely known example of this in the United States. Private campgrounds can also offer many amenities that public campgrounds do not, things like WiFi, laundry facilities, gyms, shops, and swimming pools.

It's a good idea to call the private campground or RV park ahead of time and ask whether a tent site or RV site is best for you in your SUV. Not all RV parks have spaces for tent camping, and they may not allow vehicles that aren't "real" RVs.

Realize also that campgrounds of all types generally fill up on weekends and holidays, so you may need to plan around these times in advance.

Truck stops

Truck stops are commercial rest areas that offer services for long-haul truckers. These services include gas, showers, restaurants, and spaces to park and sleep in their rigs. SUV RVers can't and shouldn't park back where the big semi trucks are, but the car parking lots in the front of these facilities can be a viable option if they allow overnight parking. One tip here is to look at the online Yelp or Google reviews of the truck stops. By doing this I've been able to find out which truck stops do and do not allow overnight parking for passenger vehicles.

Walmart parking lots

The Walmart company policy is that RVers are welcome to park overnight in their parking lots, the idea being that RVers will spend money while parked there. Sounds like the perfect place for SUV RVers, right? The problem is that the cities and towns that some Walmarts are located don't allow sleeping in a vehicle overnight, so not all Walmart stores are SUV RVer friendly.

How can you find out whether it's OK to park overnight in a Walmart parking lot? The website Walmart Locator lists (at *http://www.walmartlocator.com/no-park-walmarts/*) the Walmarts that don't allow overnight parking, but I've found that it's not comprehensive. A much better option is to download a mobile app that shows which stores allow overnight parking and which don't. Search in the app store of your choice for "Walmart overnight parking," and you should find an app that works for you.

The Walmarts that don't allow overnight parking usually have signs posted saying as much, but don't count on it. Seeing RVs already parked in the lot late in the evening can indicate that overnight parking is indeed allowed. If you're still unsure, ask a store manager if it's OK to spend the night there.

Other parking lots

I've heard from other people that overnight parking at big-box stores like Home Depot, Lowes, Sam's Club (owned by the Walmart company), and K-Mart is a good option. Grocery stores that are open 24 hours and busy restaurant parking lots can be good places to stay as well. The idea when parking in any parking lot as an SUV RVer is to look as unobtrusive as possible. Try not to call attention to yourself.

Figure 55: A free overnight parking spot/campsite at a gift shop near Arizona's Petrified Forest National Park

Many Cracker Barrel restaurants also allow overnight RV parking, as do some casinos that are eager for your gambling dollars.

Street parking

Overnight parking on the street in a city or town is another viable option for SUV RVers. I'd strongly recommend not parking in front of a house in a residential area because let's be honest, that's kind of creepy, but there are other good choices. Among these are streets in more industrial areas or business districts, streets in front of apartment complexes, streets in front of hotels, streets near college campuses (though many of these streets have stringent parking guidelines, so keep an eye out for the signs), and streets near automobile repair shops. All of these are areas in which it wouldn't be too weird to see a random vehicle parked, or there wouldn't be anyone around that would care if you were parked there.

Other places to camp

If you have friends or family members in a city and they don't have room for you to stay inside the house, ask if you can park in their driveway. I've even heard of people posting to Craigslist and asking for a (paid) place to park for the night, week, or month.

Highway rest areas or rest stops in some states are another potential place to spend the night. Doing so is illegal in some states and completely legal in others, so check beforehand what the situation is like in the state(s) you'll be passing through. For what it's worth, I know that people routinely park overnight in states where doing so is technically illegal, and they never have any problems. Try that at your own risk, but I expect the worst that would happen is that you'd be asked to move on.

New Mexico deserves a special mention here. The state offers an annual camping permit that currently costs $225 for non-New Mexico residents. It is valid for 12 months from the month of purchase and allows a year's worth of unlimited camping in New Mexico state parks. There are some nuances with this pass, however. Owning the pass means that you can stay in any "primitive" campsite (normally $8 per night without the pass) or "developed" campsite (normally $10 per night without the pass) for no extra fee. The New Mexico state parks website says, "Primitive campsites offer no special facilities except a cleared area for camping. Sites may include trash cans, chemical toilets or parking." Developed campsites offer hookups at the campsite, and if you'd like to use the hookups, it'll cost $4 to use the electric hookup, $4 to use the sewer hookup, or $8 to use both (it is free to use water hookups when they are available). So in other words, after you've got the annual camping pass, it's an extra $4 or $8 to use the hookups, and since no SUV that I know of needs a sewer hookup, it's just $4 to use the electricity if you choose to do so. It definitely makes financial sense if you'll be spending a lot of time camping in New Mexico.

One great resource for finding places to camp is the website Free Campsites (*http://freecampsites.net*). It's exactly what it sounds like. Go there, enter a location, and it will show you nearby free campsites, including BLM sites, national forest sites, casinos parking lots, and more. The website is by no means comprehensive, but I have used it several times with good results. Because the website is so popular, it's not uncommon to have company at the campsites. While this isn't a huge problem, I'd rather be alone when possible, so I try to use the website just to get an idea of where public lands are. Then I'll look on a map for dirt roads in the area that might lead to less popular camping areas.

A final resource to be aware of is Couchsurfing (*http://couchsurfing.org*). This is a website that pairs you up with people willing to let you sleep on their couch or in a spare bedroom for free. In cities and other places where legal overnight parking or camping is difficult to come by, this could be your only option.

Tips and best practices of urban/suburban camping

In places where overnight parking is of dubious legality, keep the following in mind:

1. Arrive late at night and depart early in the morning.

2. Once you park, avoid using electronic devices or anything else that will light up and that may indicate someone is inside the vehicle unless you've got really good blackout curtains.

3. Don't spend many consecutive nights in the same place. Mix up your locations if you're going to be in one town for a while.

4. Have a ready excuse or reason for why you are staying overnight in a place. A good standby is that you were driving and got tired so decided to pull over for the night.

5. Don't draw attention to your vehicle. Try to make it blend in.

6. Research potential parking places before you arrive in a city. Google Maps, Google Street View, and other similar services are great tools for this.

7. Obey local laws and posted signs.

8. Search online things like "boondocking Denver" or "overnight parking Atlanta" for the cities, towns, national parks, or other areas that you'll be passing through to see if anyone else has posted their experiences online. (Boondocking means camping outside of any sort of campground or place with hookups.) I searched for "Joshua Tree boondocking" when planning a trip to Southern California's Joshua Tree National Park and found a link to a PDF map created by the National Park Service that listed great free campsites on BLM land not too far from the park entrances. Awesome!

9. Drive around in the middle of the night in your home town to see the types of places that people park in overnight. Keep an eye out for those kinds of places when looking for a place to sleep while traveling.

10. Try not to move around too much. A vehicle that's rocking back and forth will raise eyebrows.

Leave no trace

I am a lifelong lover of the outdoors. Indeed, the main reason I travel in my SUV is that I want to spend more time in our country's amazing deserts and mountains. Over the years, I've hiked thousands of miles, scaled more than a hundred mountains, and completed more than a thousand rock climbs. To say that nature is important to me is a gross understatement. Few things give me more joy than parking my SUV somewhere wild and feeling like I am the only person on earth. Conversely, few things infuriate me more than parking in one of these seemingly pristine and wild places and stepping out of my vehicle only to find the ground littered with beer cans, bullet casings, chunks of cardboard, strips of toilet paper, and other pieces of manmade detritus.

"Leave no trace" is a mantra espoused by many of us who love the outdoors, from young Boy Scouts to new age hippies. It's a set of principles that guide us in our outdoor pursuits, with the overall theme being that we should leave no impact on the land after we've enjoyed it. I have adapted leave no trace principles (as outlined by the Leave No Trace Center for Outdoor Ethics, a nonprofit dedicated to educating people on how to reduce their environmental impact) to make them specifically applicable to SUV RVers, and they are outlined below. While we normally think of "the outdoors" as beautiful places out in nature, I'll expand the definition to include any place that we visit or spend a night.

1. Plan ahead – To the best of your ability, figure out where you're going to go before you get there. Have a potential campsite in mind so that you don't have to drive all over the place looking for one. Educate yourself so that you know how to minimize your impact on a given environment. Know what plants and animals you need to be aware of.

2. Choose your campsites wisely – Camp on hard, previously-used surfaces. Don't drive out into that pristine meadow when there's an established campsite right next to it. Don't drive places where roads don't exist.

3. Don't litter – Pack out any trash you produce, and try to pack out any other trash that you see. Leave your campsite cleaner than you found it. If you're going to defecate naturally in the outdoors, do it far from water sources. Dig a hole at least six inches deep and do your business into the hole. Cover it up afterward, and pack out any used toilet paper in Ziploc bags (or burn it if appropriate). If you're into guns and shooting, don't leave targets, clay pigeons, bullet casings, or shells on the ground. As the saying goes, take nothing but photos and leave nothing but footprints.

4. Don't alter the landscape – Don't dig a big ol' trench around your tent or SUV. Don't hammer nails into trees. Don't disturb or remove Native American artifacts. Don't create and leave walls or rings of rocks. Do, to the best of your ability, make the place look more natural than you found it. Don't chop down live trees for firewood. Don't clear brush.

5. Minimize the effects of campfires – Only have campfires when and where permitted. Make fires in existing fire pits or rings. Question whether you really need a campfire at all. Know that in tightly spaced campgrounds, having a campfire can negatively impact those around you. Some people with respiratory issues can't stay in campgrounds because there's just too much smoke for them. Don't enjoy your experience at someone else's expense.

6. Don't mess with wildlife – Don't feed, trap, or otherwise harass wild animals. One more time: Do not feed the wildlife. This includes birds, squirrels, and other cute little critters. Don't leave your food out where animals can easily get it. Be especially vigilant in bear country.

7. Be considerate of others – Don't play loud music. Don't let your dog run wild and bother other people. Don't run a generator near other campers. Don't take up more room than you have to. Don't break the rules and ruin things for everyone else. Don't be a jerk.

Finally, practice the golden rule of the outdoors: Leave a place as you would like to find it.

6. Food and Cooking

To see additional relevant links for this chapter, visit http://suvrving.com/book/six/.

The sheer variety of offerings in any bookstore or library's cooking section attests to the fact that it's difficult to talk about something so necessary and personal as food in a way that would apply and appeal to everyone. In this chapter, I will simply cover the things that you need to be aware of as an SUV RVer, including refrigeration, going stoveless, and cooking.

Refrigeration

The real question you need to ask yourself first is whether you need to keep food or drinks cold at all. If not, you save yourself having to deal with (or purchase) either a cooler or refrigerator. Can you buy cold drinks instead of bringing them with you? Can you leave drinks outside or in a stream to keep them cool instead? Can you eat foods that don't require refrigeration?

If you do need to keep items cool when you're on the go as an SUV RVer, you've got two options: a cooler or a refrigerator. Both coolers and portable refrigerators are big, heavy, and bulky. Coolers are good because they don't require electricity. They are simple to use and don't have fancy, delicate moving parts that can break (though they do still have some moving parts). The downside is that they won't keep things cold for more than a couple of days unless you get a very high quality, multi-hundred-dollar model from a company like Yeti or Pelican.

If you want to increase the efficacy of a cooler, consider covering either the inside or outside with extra foam insulation. I cut up a cheap camping sleeping pad to give extra insulation to the little portable cooler that I sometimes take with me.

Blocks of ice will last longer than bags of ice cubes. Freeze bottles of water to create your own smaller ice blocks. This can also be done with rinsed milk jugs or juice bottles. And the key to getting any type of ice to last longer is to minimize the number of openings and closings (and therefore the letting in of warmer air) of the cooler. The less you open the cooler, the longer the ice will last. Keeping your cooler out of direct sunlight also helps.

One thing to remember is that while ice is relatively inexpensive, it's not free. It's easy to go through a dollar's worth of ice a day. If you'll be SUV RVing for months or years at a time, spending the money on a refrigerator and battery setup to power it may not be so economically unreasonable, though this does introduce its own set of challenges (as outlined below).

I would stay away from things marketed as "electric coolers." These are essentially just coolers with fans in them and aren't satisfactory substitutes for refrigerators.

Portable refrigerators are made for truckers, RVers, and boaters. They work just like regular home refrigerators do, but they are generally much smaller (starting from about the size of a small cooler) and can run off of 12-volt battery systems. Portable refrigerators are expensive (usually around $400 and up) and require a whole lot of energy to run. You'd need a substantial deep cycle battery bank to keep one of these things going in an SUV (more on this shortly). I have no experience with this kind of refrigerator in my SUV and am mentioning it here only so that you can look into it more on your own if it sounds like something that would work for you. If there's a good chance that a refrigerator would make SUV RV life more enjoyable for you, especially if you like to cook, then be aware of the costs involved and space requirements.

I occasionally will take a small cooler with me when I go on trips in the heat of the summer, but even then I just keep drinks in it. I'll take bottles of Gatorade, freeze them before the trip, and stick the frozen-solid bottles in the cooler. When I pop open the cooler a couple of days later after a long, hot day of hiking in the mountains, the bottles are still partially frozen and slushy. It's like having a Slurpee machine in my SUV.

Even though I generally don't use a refrigerator or cooler, I still need a place to put the stuff that I'm going to eat. For this I use two smallish plastic bins. When stacked on top of each other, these bins fit perfectly on the floor in the space behind the front passenger seat and in front of the rear bench seat. I've found that two separate bins are easier to manage than one larger, heavier one, and having two bins keeps things nicely separated. I usually put perishables (bread, fruit, etc.) in one and non-perishables (cans, granola bars, etc.) in the other. No one bin gets so heavy that it's a pain to move.

The best way to store food items is to take them out of the cardboard boxes they come in. This cuts down on the amount of space that they take up. If you eat a lot of fruit and vegetables, consider storing them in a mesh bag and hanging the bag from somewhere in your vehicle to keep them fresh.

Going stoveless

Going stoveless means eating foods that don't require cooking or, ideally, refrigeration. This is a great route for SUV RVers to go because it means you won't have to carry a stove or worry about finding the right places or weather conditions for cooking your food. Even if you love cooking or can't go without hot food, it's good to have or at least know about the stoveless options for those times when you run out of cooking fuel or simply don't feel like cooking.

So how is it possible to eat without a stove? The easiest option is simply to eat out for every meal. I call this credit card RVing, and it is obviously the most expensive option. It would cost about $10 to $15 a day minimum to eat like this if you stuck to fast food or prepared grocery store eats, and the sky's the limit at the upper end of the price spectrum.

If you are unable or unwilling to eat out for every meal, there are still plenty of stoveless options for you. There are a number of foods that require no refrigeration to store or heat to prepare, and I've listed some of them below by category.

Perishables

These items can be stored for short periods of time in your vehicle, depending on the temperature inside. If conditions are too unfavorable for storing them, you can still buy them from markets or grocery stores to eat right away.

- Fruit: apples, oranges, bananas, avocados, pears, peaches, plums, mangos, melons, tamarinds, berries, etc.
- Vegetables: carrots, tomatoes (I know, I know, it's technically a fruit...), peppers
- Cheese (especially the harder cheeses)
- Bagels
- Pita bread
- Tortillas
- Rolls
- Loaves of bread – Harder breads like pumpernickel and rye last longer.
- Salads

Spreadables

Eat these by the spoonful or put them on top of other things like bread, fruit, tortillas, and crackers.

- Peanut butter and other nut butters (almond, sunflower, cashew, pistachio, blends, etc.)
- Nutella
- Vegemite
- Soybean spread
- Tahini
- Olive paste
- Sun-dried tomato paste
- Anchovy paste
- Umami paste

- Pesto
- Individual hummus packets

Seeds, nuts, etc.

- Nuts: peanuts, walnuts, cashews, almonds, pistachios, pecans, nut mixes
- Seeds: pumpkin seeds, flax seed, sunflower seeds, chia seeds, seed mixes
- GORP/trail mix

Bars

- Granola bars
- Nut bars
- Energy bars, including protein bars, meal replacement bars, etc.

Dried fruits and vegetables

- Apricots
- Raisins
- Cranberries
- Apples
- Pineapples
- Mangos
- Dates
- Figs
- Wasabi peas
- Fruit leathers

Meats

- Jerky of various flavors and from various animals
- Sausage, pepperoni, summer sausage, salami, smoked sausage, cooked bacon
- Foil packets of tuna, tuna salad, salmon, Spam, or chicken
- Anchovies
- Pâté

Recipes and mixes

- Muesli/granola with powdered milk (just add water)
- Cereal with powdered milk and water
- Sandwiches: vegetable and cheese, peanut butter with jelly/banana/honey/Nutella, etc.

Chips, crackers, etc.

- Kale chips
- Tortilla chips

- Potato chips
- Other chips (Fritos, Doritos, Cheetos, etc.)
- Saltine crackers
- Goldfish crackers
- Cheez-Its
- Pretzels, pretzel bites
- Ritz crackers (good with nut butters, honey, Nutella, etc.)
- Rice cakes

Dehydrated just-add-water bases

Even if you don't have hot water, you can add room-temperature water to these dry foods to create meals of varying palatability. If you want to get fancy, find an empty peanut butter jar or something similar, put the water and dry food inside, and set the jar in the sun for a couple of hours.

- Oatmeal (can add cut-up apples, peanut butter, honey, chocolate, dried fruit, Craisins, etc.)
- Couscous
- Hummus
- Quinoa
- Instant pudding
- Instant potatoes
- Refried beans

Sweets

- Pastries
- Breakfast pasties (e.g., Pop Tarts)
- Candy: chocolate, candy bars, hard candies, sour candies, etc.
- Pudding
- Cookies (including Oreos, Fig Newtons, etc.)
- Fruit snacks
- Things like pretzels, nuts, and dried fruits covered in chocolate or yogurt
- Shortbread

Other

- Energy chews, gels, etc.
- MREs – These are often not ideal without a heat source.
- Dehydrated meals – Again, not ideal without a heat source.
- Protein shakes (in liquid or powdered form)
- Other powdered drinks: Gatorade, lemonade, apple cider, etc.
- Canned foods – If there are canned foods that you like that don't need to be heated up, they can be great for stoveless SUV RVing. Olives come to mind

immediately. Depending on your taste buds, things like beans or chili may also fall into this category.

Note: Remember that condiments like mayonnaise, mustard and ketchup come in individually wrapped, disposable packets that do not have to be refrigerated. And cheese does not need to be refrigerated for several days. So peanut butter and jelly/banana/honey/Nutella sandwiches, as well as cheese, tuna, BLT, and chicken salad sandwiches, etc. are easy, stoveless meals.

Stoveless tips

Combine items from the above lists to create your own entrees—hummus, crackers, and olives, for example, or tortillas, refried beans, fresh tomatoes, and Fritos, or canned chili over bread.

Keep an eye on the amount of sugar and sodium you're consuming, as a lot of these pre-packaged products are particularly high in these two areas.

Try out individual items or travel-sized portions from retailers specializing in selling individual and travel-sized items (Minimus at *http://minimus.biz* is one I've used). For example, you can buy a single packet of honey for $0.18 or a packet of hummus spread for $0.96. Once you've found items you like, consider buying in bulk from places like Amazon, Sam's Club, or Costco.

Walk through your favorite grocery store and browse each aisle. Pick out things to try out prior to going stoveless for a more extended period of time. You'll be surprised at how many foods do not require refrigeration or cooking and can be considered part of a well-balanced meal.

So why shouldn't everyone go stoveless? Well, one potential downside to stoveless eating is that it can be more expensive, because let's face it, everything is more expensive than heating up ramen, boiling potatoes, or frying up eggs. Another downside is that in cold weather it can be really nice to have a hot meal, and a stoveless meal will not be hot. The final downside is that while stoveless cuisine can be broad and varied, by definition it will never be as broad and varied as the options you have with a stove.

Cooking

If you like to cook or if you want to eat more than what a stoveless diet can give you, you'll need a stove, pots, pans, plates, bowls, and utensils. When buying these items, consider what you will actually use them for (not what you aspire to use them for), and try to buy small or compact versions when possible. Remember that space is your most precious commodity. Guard it every way you can!

Where to cook

First let's talk about where exactly you'll be cooking. Is it safe to cook inside the vehicle? Possibly, but there are a few different dangers to be aware of. For the SUV RVer, the SUV itself essentially becomes a mobile, hard-sided tent. Just as you wouldn't use a camp stove inside of a tent, you probably don't want to use one inside of your SUV.

The first danger is from fire. Even a large SUV is a relatively confined space (to say nothing of the smaller vehicles), so the roof and sides of the SUV, the seats, and the things you've packed inside the vehicle will never be too far away from the flame you'd be using for cooking. All of those things are flammable. It would be all-too-easy for the stove to get too close to something or for you to accidently knock the stove over. For this reason alone, I do not recommend cooking with an open flame inside of an SUV. If you do choose to do it, having a smoke alarm and a fire extinguisher handy is a good idea.

Another big reason to not cook inside the vehicle is that burning stoves create carbon monoxide, the same deadly stuff that your vehicle's engine gives off that can kill you. I have a carbon monoxide detector in my SUV and recommend that all SUV RVers do the same. If you do decide to cook inside, make sure there is plenty of ventilation in the form of open windows, open doors, and a fan or two.

If those reasons aren't enough to dissuade you from cooking inside the vehicle, think of the smells. Sure, that chicken tikka masala will taste delicious, but do you really want your SUV to smell like that until the end of time? The

Figure 56. Heating up a can of soup on an SUV's rear bumper with a small camp stove. The stove is surrounded by a lightweight windscreen.

soft, cushy interior of your vehicle will soak up those odors like a sponge.

It is not uncommon for people who live or travel in vans to cook inside them. These vans are much larger than SUVs, so there is more room to cook safely. In addition, these vans usually have better ventilation in the form of roof vents and fans.

So if we probably won't be cooking inside an SUV, where will we cook? One common method is to open up the back of the vehicle and cook there. This lets you still access things that are stored inside the vehicle (pots, pans, paper towels, etc.) while safely cooking outside.

If the rear door of your SUV opens upward, great! You've got built-in rain protection. If the rear door of your SUV opens to the side, great! You've got built-in wind protection. In either case, a tarp used as an awning can keep you dry while you cook in inclement weather and cool while you cook on sunny days.

People who camp out of their pickup trucks often use the tailgate as a table on which to prepare foods and place the stove. SUVs don't have anything like that, so we SUV RVers have to find another option. One is to use the top of the rear bumper if doing so makes sense. My SUV has a flat top/step on top of the rear bumper that is about 8 inches (20 centimeters) deep when the rear door is open, and I've cooked on that many times. (See Figure 56.)

Another possibility is to use a small table (like a camp table or folding laptop desk) or other object that you've already got in your vehicle like a hard-topped bin or box. Whatever you use needs to be flat-topped and stable. Cooking like this can be done to the sides or rear of your vehicle.

The third option is a good one if you have something heavy like a big bin in the back of your vehicle. The idea here is to get a flat board or piece of wood to act as a cantilevered table. One end of the tabletop is weighed down by the bin or whatever the heavy object in the back of your SUV is, and the other end sticks out from the back of the SUV and overhangs the ground. For things like chopping vegetables, the board would need to be either be held down by something very heavy inside the SUV or be supported by a drop-down leg or two.

The final option is to simply cook on the ground somewhere near your vehicle. It may not be pretty, but it doesn't require an extra stuff. Humans have been cooking on the ground for as long as there have been humans. This would be more enjoyable if you had one of those stadium-style portable padded seats (as popularized by the company Crazy Creek) to make sitting on the ground more comfortable.

That covers all of the areas in and around your vehicle where you can cook, but another option is to find a place with picnic tables. This is an especially good idea if it's raining outside, as many places have picnic tables under roofs or awnings. Spots where you can often find picnic tables include highway rest areas, neighborhood parks, city parks, county parks, state parks, national parks, recreation areas, some popular trailheads, and campgrounds.

Stoves

Portable stoves come in several different form factors, and these are often dictated by the type and size of fuel canister used. I will break liquid-fuel stoves down into three basic form factors: the backpacking stove, the car camping stove, and the expedition stove. (See Figure 57.)

The **backpacking stove** is what I call the form factor that has the fuel canister standing upright with the stove mechanism or burner attached on top of that. It is the type of stove that I recommend for most SUV RVers who don't cook much because of their low cost, ease of use, and small size.

The first propane stove that I bought and referred to above was this type of stove, but far more common is the smaller second stove I mentioned that runs off of the liquid fuel mixture that comes in smaller canisters. Propane canisters are cheaper and probably more widely available, but they are heavy and bulky. The smaller mixed liquid fuel canisters are a bit more expensive and maybe a little bit harder to find (though still relatively easy; they're at most Walmarts and larger sporting goods stores) but are much more compact. Either way, these backpacking stoves can be relatively inexpensive. The small one that I now use set me back less than $10. I don't cook much, but I do use the stove to heat up cans of soup and pots of water, and I'm surprised at just how long the fuel canisters last. The canister I'm currently using has been used to heat up fifteen cans of soup, boil three small pots of water, and cook one meal (when I loaned the stove to a neighboring camper), and it's still about a quarter full. I use a

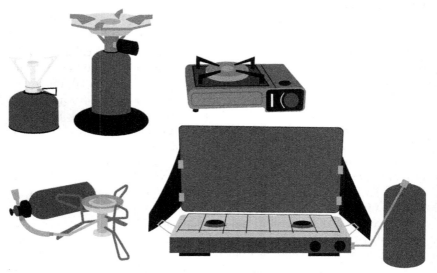

Figure 57. The different form factors of stove options for SUV RVers. Clockwise from top left: a backpacking stove using an isobutene/propane/butane mix fuel canister, a backpacking stove using a propane canister, a one-burner butane car camping stove, a two-burner propane car camping stove, an expedition stove.

permanent marker to tally on the bottom of the canister how much use I'm getting out of the canister.

The downside of the backpacking stove form factor is that because the stove is long and tall, it is easier to tip over, resulting in a spilled meal at best and a fiery vehicle at worst. As long as you are careful, this shouldn't be a problem, but it is something to be aware of. If you're really worried about tipping your stove over, you can buy little legs that attach to the fuel canister and provide more stability (search online for "fuel canister stand").

What I call the **car camping stove** form factor is much flatter than the backpacking stove. You would not bring this stove on a multi-day hike because of its size and weight. Instead of being long and tall, it is wide and flat, and therefore much harder to tip over. Some of these stoves run on propane while others run on butane. Butane canisters are perhaps the most difficult of all of the fuel canisters to find, but they're not exactly rare, either. Just buy a few at a time when you do see them and you'll be fine. The butane stoves tend to have a single burner while the propane stoves usually have two burners. If you routinely cook for more than a couple of people or prepare more involved meals, a two-burner propane stove is a good choice. Of course, with the larger propane stoves come the larger bulk of the fuel canisters and the stoves themselves.

What I call the **expedition stove** was designed to be used in a wide variety of conditions on things like mountaineering expeditions and round-the-world bicycle journeys. These stoves burn just about any liquid fuel, including white gas, kerosene, and gasoline. The tradeoff is that they are a bit more finicky and complicated than any of the above-mentioned stoves. If you already have a stove like this laying around, by all means go ahead and use it, but I don't think it's the best choice for SUV RVers unless you are spending a lot of time out in the boondocks or doing a lot of international travel. I've always found this type of stove particularly difficult to operate, and I would never use one inside of a vehicle because of the possibilities of flare-ups and spilled fuel. Some of these stoves will also work with widely available fuel canisters, making them a bit easier to use and even more flexible.

For all of these stoves, regardless of the type, I prefer ones that have built-in piezo ignition systems, though I do keep a small lighter packed with my stove just in case the igniter fails.

There are a few other types of camp stove that I'll mention briefly. You can buy **wood-burning camp stoves** that run off of twigs, leaves, pinecones, and small branches. So what's not to like? Fuel is free and abundant, right? Yes, it is free, but it is not necessarily abundant. You'll be hard pressed to find enough fuel in the desert or after rain, for example. Also, because a stove like this throws off embers, it is likely illegal to use in dry areas that are at high risk for fires. Some campsites and areas also explicitly state that gathering wood is prohibited.

Canned heat stoves are inexpensive and simple to operate. The fuel source is canned heat, often referred to by the brand name Sterno. You open up a can, light the fuel inside, and set the can on the stove under the potholders. Simple. You can't adjust the flame or heat on these stoves, which somewhat limits their practicality for cooking. I've also heard people complain that the flame isn't strong enough to boil water, which would limit its use to things like heating up soups. The only thing I've used a Sterno can for is roasting marshmallows for s'mores, and it worked great for that.

Finally, **solid fuel stoves** (usually called Esbit stoves) are an option. These stoves burn small tablets or cubes of hexamine. Just set the cube on the stove (which is usually just some variation of a simple metal platform) and light it with a match or lighter. I've never used these stoves or this kind of fuel, so I can only say what I've read about them. These stoves are extremely lightweight and simple. A single tablet will burn for approximately 12 minutes, according to reports, and boil 500 ml. (about 17 ounces) of water in about 8 minutes. As with canned heat, there's not really any way to regulate the heat once the fuel is burning, though again, this might not be an issue for you if all you need to do is boil water, warm up MREs, or heat soups and stews. The extremely compact size, light weight (less than an ounce in some cases!), low cost, and ease of use are the main benefits of this kind of stove. Esbit fuel also reportedly has an odor to it that is especially noticeable in more confined spaces like a tent vestibule. So on top of all previous warnings against cooking inside an SUV, definitely don't do it with an Esbit stove unless you want all of your upholstery impregnated with that distinct odor.

Definitely keep size in mind when selecting a stove. For example, the first stove I bought for my SUV RVing adventures ran off of the one-pound, dark green propane cylinders that are inexpensive and readily available at big-box stores and sporting goods stores. The cylinders were big and bulky, as was the stove itself. Together, the fuel canisters and stove took up a significant amount of room, more room than I was willing to sacrifice given how little actual cooking I do. After doing some more research into what was on the market, I found a stove the size of a small medicine bottle that runs off of much smaller isobutane/propane/butane mixture fuel canisters that are made for backpacking. This was a great space-saving choice.

Regardless of the stove you use, either buy a wind screen for it (if it's a smaller stove) or make sure it has one built in (if it's one of the larger car camping stoves). A stove without a windscreen in windy conditions is far less fuel-efficient than one with a windscreen. If cooking inside your vehicle or in close proximity to your vehicle to the side or behind it, think about splashes. Your boiling stew or sizzling stir-fry may boil, splat, spit, and crackle its way onto whatever is around the pot or pan it's in. A folding splash guard (or tall windscreen) can keep this from affecting anything around it, as can simply cooking away from anything that could potentially be marred by splashes.

Be sure that your stove has cooled to a safe temperature before putting it away. You don't want it melting or burning anything, including your fingers.

Unconventional cooking methods

An **immersion water heater** is an unconventional form of cooking, but it does the job if all you want to do is heat up some water for soups, hot drinks, or instant noodles. An immersion water heater looks like a funny curling iron that you stick into a mug of water or liquid and wait while the heating coils boil the water. There are 12-volt versions of these gadgets that plug into a car's power outlet (i.e., the cigarette lighter socket). Try using one of these in your driveway at home first to make sure it works for you and doesn't blow a fuse in your SUV while you're out in the middle of nowhere. These heaters are best used with glass or ceramic mugs and may melt plastic ones.

Grilling and **barbecuing** can be fantastic ways to cook on the road. Many campsites, picnic areas, and parks have barbecue grills available for people to use, so you don't even have to haul your own around. If you grill often, there are both charcoal and propane grills small enough to travel with.

I don't know much about **solar ovens** except that there are folding, portable versions that RVers can take on their travels. This could be a good way to cook if your travels take you to sunnier climes or if you frequent areas where fires are not allowed.

A **lunch box stove** is a rectangular box about the size of a lunch box and is plugged into the SUV's 12-volt power outlet. This kind of stove is great for heating up things like burritos, sandwiches, and pizza slices.

Foil dinners have been a staple of campers for decades and are an option if you'll be having a wood campfire. Foil dinners can also potentially be placed under the hood on top of the engine block of a running vehicle, though I've heard that this type of cooking works less well these days than in decades past due to modern car engines not getting as hot to the touch. Still, the prospect of plopping dinner under the hood, driving around, and arriving at your destination with dinner fully cooked sounds pretty nice, doesn't it? If it works for you and your vehicle, there is a book called *Manifold Destiny: The One! The Only! Guide to Cooking on Your Car Engine!* that might be worth a look.

Gas stations often let you use their **microwaves** if you've bought something there, as might some grocery stores that have little dining areas in them (usually close to the deli section).

Thermos cooking is an option that looks like it would be great for SUV RVers. It involves boiling water and then putting it in a thermos along with food that you want to cook. You set the thermos aside and let the hot water cook whatever food is inside (beans, rice, oats, lentils, etc.) for a few hours. This saves on fuel and cooks the food while you're doing other things.

My kitchen items

I started off keeping all of my cooking supplies in a small plastic bin about the size of a shoebox. There was nothing wrong with this setup other than that it

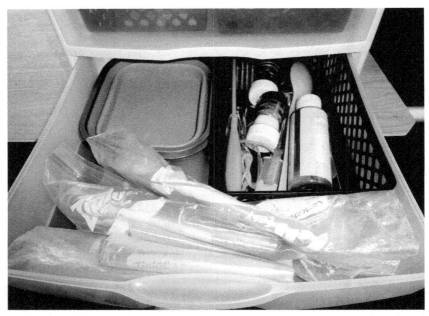

Figure 58. The kitchen drawer in the three-drawer plastic bin

Figure 59. Rear view of the plastic drawer unit with metal rack in which I keep a small pot (with two small cups and backpacking stove nested inside), plastic dinner plate, foldable windscreen, and fuel canister

was another object floating freely around in my SUV. I have since moved most kitchen items over to one of the drawers of the plastic unit that I keep on top of the rear shelf of my SUV. (See Figure 58.)

On the back of the plastic drawer unit, I've attached a metal basket made to fit on the inside of a kitchen cabinet door. (See Figure 59.) That's where I keep items that are too large to keep inside of the drawer, namely a small pot (with two nesting cups and backpacking stove inside of it), plate, windscreen, and fuel canister.

Here's a list of what I keep in the drawer:

- Collapsible bowl
- Serrated knife
- Non-serrated knife
- Spoon, fork, butter knife
- Long-handled spoon
- Potholder – I use this less for grabbing a hot pot and more as a safe surface on which to place a hot pot.
- Small double-sided spice shaker with salt and pepper
- Small double-sided spice shaker with red chili powder and curry powder
- Liquid soap in a small bottle
- Tiny can opener and mini lighter on a lanyard
- Ziploc bags of varying sizes

I used to also have a small cutting board but found that I didn't use it enough to warrant taking it with me everywhere.

You'll see that my kitchen supplies are tailored to fit my needs and desires (i.e., trying to cook as little as possible). There are common kitchen items like a big pot, frying pan, measuring cups, spatula, and serving spoon that I don't need but that might be essential for you. Other possible items include a wok, potato masher, camp stove toaster, Dutch oven, various lids, and coffee maker. You might also want different spices, or you might want to pack things like cooking oil or olive oil. You know your kitchen needs better than I do.

If you cook a lot and want to get really fancy, you can make a chuck box. (See Figure 60.) This is a camp kitchen in a box that you can set atop picnic tables or have accessible from one of your SUV's open doors. A chuck box is usually homemade and designed and created specifically for the needs of a specific individual or group (e.g., a family or Boy Scout troop). These boxes open up to reveal cubbies and spaces for things like fuel, utensils, cookware, stove, Ziploc bags, spices, and condiments, and napkins or paper towels. The stove can be removed from inside the box and placed on top of the box or on a slide-out shelf for easier use. A good chuck box fits in the space you have available and is easy to add to and remove from your vehicle for day-to-day use and storage.

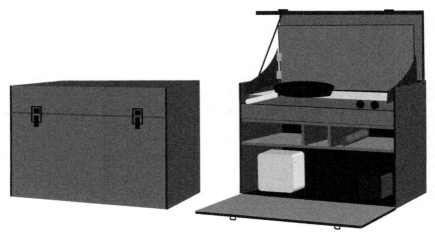

Figure 60. A chuck box or camp kitchen in a box when closed (left) and open (right)

What to cook

I am no chef. I dislike cooking and try to avoid it whenever possible, both at home and on the road. As such, I'm really not the best person to be giving advice on what to be cooking. Take the advice I do give with a grain of salt and season it with your own needs and experiences.

When I do cook while SUV RVing, it's usually just to heat up soup, stew, or other canned delicacy. With a now near-infinite number of foods and variations to choose from on the market, ranging from super-processed to super-organic, it's easy to find canned foods for any diet. Canned foods include soups, stews, chilies, beans, pastas, and vegetables. As with the prepackaged stoveless foods, be sure to keep an eye on the amount of sodium in these canned foods, as it is usually very high. You can make these canned foods go further by eating them with rice, quinoa, or bread (including rolls, bagels, and tortillas).

Cleaning the cookware and utensils

So how does one do the dishes when SUV RVing? As with many aspects of SUV RVing, it can be as simple or complicated as you want. On the simple end of the spectrum is using disposable flatware, utensils, and paper towels. Just throw them away and you're done. This method minimizes the use of your valuable water supply, though it does increase the amount of trash you generate.

On the other end of the spectrum is a kitchen sink. Literally. If you have the space in your SUV and the desire to make things feel more like they do at home, you could create a sink system complete with running water. It could be as basic as a wooden frame with a wooden top on which you could mount a bar or RV sink with a hand pump faucet (these have little levers or buttons that draw the water up when pulled or pressed and are often used in RVs and on boats). Then underneath the sink would be two big plastic water jugs, one holding fresh water and one holding the used water. The hand pump on the faucet pulls water up from the fresh water jug and dispenses it out the faucet. The used water then goes down into the sink and down the drain, and tubing from the sink carries it directly to the second water jug. (See Figure 61.)

No electricity or external hookups would be required for a setup like this, although you could add an electric pump if you so desired. You could place this sink unit inside the rear hatch/door of your SUV, at one of the side doors (and accessible from the outside), or along the inside wall of your SUV (feasible only if you have a large SUV or one that is set up to sleep a single person). A good alternative to storing it on the inside of your vehicle would be to store it on a cargo hitch carrier. And if you wanted to extend the "countertop" of your sink box a bit further, you could mount your stove in the countertop and then put all of your kitchen items under the stove and make a single sink, stove, chuck box unit. This way your entire kitchen setup would be out of the way of your sleeping space inside the vehicle yet still easily accessible when it's time to cook or clean up.

If all of that sounds like a nightmare to deal with, there are other kitchen cleanup solutions that take up far less space and require much less attention. Paper towels (or a sponge or washcloth if you'd prefer something reusable) and a spray bottle will clean just about any pot or dish. Adding a 1-to-1 white vinegar and water solution to the spray bottle will make it an even better cleaning agent that will break up grease. I've found that turning the nozzle of the spray bottle to the "stream" mode instead of the "mist" mode makes a powerful little blast that is good for attacking stubborn foodstuffs clinging to your dishes and the bottom of

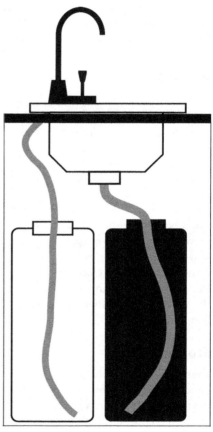

Figure 61. Diagram of a simple sink setup. When the hand pump next to the sink is engaged, water is drawn up from the white freshwater jug, pushed out through the faucet, and drained down out of the sink into the black jug of used water.

pots and pans. If you do a lot of cooking, a scrub brush might be a good investment. Non-soapy wet wipes can also help with cleaning off dishes. If you're washing a lot of dishes, a sink of some sort that you can fill with water would be useful. An empty plastic bin or a collapsible sink made for camping would do the job well.

Note that if you cook a lot with raw meat and eggs, you'll definitely want to wash your dishes with soap; a simple wipe with a paper towel won't be sufficient.

To dry your cookware and utensils, leave them out in the sun for a bit or at least leave them out in your SUV or other place where they can air dry. Don't put them back into a storage bin, drawer, or bag while they're still wet. I recommend not leaving them outside unsupervised or overnight as bugs and animals might be attracted to the smells left over from the food. Nobody wants to use forks that have been licked by raccoons.

Water

One of the great joys of SUV RVing for me is getting away from everything and going out into the middle of nowhere for a few days. Perhaps the single most important bit of preparation I do for these trips is making sure I have enough water for my drinking, eating, bathing, and dental hygiene needs. Put simply, you will have a very, very bad time if you run out of water.

How much water do you need? This depends on a variety of factors, including weather conditions (heat, humidity, sun/shade), the amount of water you tend to drink, whether you need water for cooking and cleaning, how long you'll be away from water sources, your bathing habits (e.g., you'll need a lot more water for showering than for wiping yourself down with wet wipes), and how physically active you are. To maintain proper hydration in normal temperature and activity conditions, health authorities recommend drinking at least two liters (roughly half a gallon) of water a day, and all other water needs should be added to that. It's definitely better to have too much water available than too little.

Storing water

There is really just one way to store water, and that's to put it in a jug or container of some sort, but the type of jug or container you put it in can vary from the thin plastic bottles you can get at the grocery store to heavy-duty, military-grade jugs and cans. I use the one-gallon grocery store water jugs and then just fill them up again with tap water when they're empty. I prefer having several of these smaller water jugs instead of one or two really big ones. They are easier to handle (i.e., lighter and less cumbersome) than the big 5- or 6-gallon ones, plus they're easier to store in the SUV because I can put one or two in the random smaller spaces I have instead of having to carve out a big chunk of space for the large jug. Moreover, I can take the exact amount of water I need for a trip; it's easier to deal in one-gallon multiples instead of 5-gallon ones. I also like that the grocery store bottles, unlike the military-grade jugs, are clear, meaning that I can easily see exactly how much water I have left.

I know that some people simply buy large packs of 35 or 64 disposable bottles of water for each trip. If you do this, be sure to recycle the empty bottles.

And of course you can have a mixture of large jugs and smaller bottles as you see fit. In addition to the one-gallon jugs I use, I usually have a handful of one-liter and 16-ounce bottles for hiking and using around camp.

Getting water

You can obviously buy jugs or bottles of water at any market, store, or gas station that you come across. If you already have containers for the water, you can fill your own jugs at home or on the road. A great option is to use water refill stations. These are made for the 5-gallon jugs that you fill and keep in your home as drinking water, but most of the machines work with any water jug. As of this writing, water from these machines is roughly 30 to 40 cents a gallon. Big-box stores, grocery stores, and gas stations often have these refill stations.

You can fill up your water for free at campgrounds or parks. If a campground doesn't have water at each campsite, there are often spigots spread throughout the campground or near the bathrooms. At public parks, look for outside faucets near the toilets or for faucets attached to stand-alone drinking fountains. National park visitor centers and ranger stations will also often have outside spigots for visitors to use. Sometimes you can even get water at the sinks in laundromats (ask permission first). A length of flexible tubing (such as a section of new garden hose that's safe for drinking water) can help you get water from a bathroom sink faucet or a drinking fountain into your larger jugs or containers.

You'll see some outdoor faucets that have been painted red. The red means that the water is not potable and is unsafe to drink.

It's never a bad idea to get a free cup of water when ordering food from a fast food restaurant. It's not much, but it can make your cache of stored water last a bit longer.

If you will be camping or traveling near water sources, you may not have to take much water with you at all, but all water from lakes, streams, and other bodies of water should first be boiled (keep it at a rolling boil for one minute to kill the bad stuff), filtered, or treated with chemicals like iodine or chlorine. Backpacking filters can work well but be sure to compare filter flow rates before buying one. I have a very small and light filter that is great for ultralight backpacking, but it takes 5 to 8 minutes to get just one liter of filtered water through it. I'm also a big fan of gravity filters. You can fill up a bag of unfiltered water, hang it up from a tree or your vehicle's roof rack, and let gravity do the work of sending water from the bag through the in-line filter and into another clean water bottle or bag.

7. Toilets and Bathing

To see additional relevant links for this chapter, visit http://suvrving.com/book/seven/.

Going to the bathroom and keeping clean are probably the first two question marks in people's minds when they hear about SUV RVing, but don't worry. They are both relatively easy issues to solve.

Going to the bathroom
Public facilities

Put bluntly, the less I have to deal with my own poop, the better. I've found that the best and easiest way to do my business when SUV RVing is to use real, flushing toilets whenever possible, including at the following locations:

- Campgrounds
- Visitor centers
- Parks
- Rest stops
- Grocery stores
- Libraries
- Gas stations
- Restaurants (especially fast food restaurants)
- Coffee shops
- Museums
- Movie theaters
- Laundromats
- Churches

The problem is that these places are obviously only as useful as their proximity to you. If you're boondocking out in the middle of the desert, knowing that you can go to the bathroom at a grocery store doesn't do you any good. My suggestion is to make sure you stop and use the facilities in the last town you go through before entering the forest, mountains, desert, parking lot, or wherever else you'll be camping.

Portable flush toilets

If you want to take some of the comforts of a real bathroom on the road with you, a commercially available portable flush toilet may be what you're looking for. These smallish, usually square or rectangular toilets are made for boats, RVs, and tents. They usually have two tanks in them: a water tank and a waste (black water) tank. After using the toilet, you press a button or pull a lever on the side and fresh water from the water tank washes everything down into the waste tank. Liquid deodorant is placed in the tanks to keep smells down. When the waste tank is full, it gets emptied out at an RV dump station (search online for "free RV dump stations") or vault toilet.

You might figure out a way to use a portable toilet inside of a large SUV, but I wouldn't recommend that for odor reasons. If you want one of these, your best bet is to use it outside of your vehicle at your campsite. Other disadvantages of portable flush toilets include the need for a lot of water, their relative complexity (compared to other off-grid toilets, which we'll get to shortly), their relatively large size and substantial weight, and the unpleasantness of emptying out the black water tank.

Portable non-flush toilets

"Dry" toilets are smaller, cheaper, and simpler to operate than portable flush toilets, though they somehow feel decidedly less civilized than even the portable flushing toilets. One version of this kind of commode is the bucket toilet. You line a bucket (anywhere from two to five gallons in capacity, depending on your needs; a smaller-capacity one might actually be small enough to let you set it on top of a seat in your vehicle to use if you're short) with a plastic trash bag and sprinkle in some kitty litter. Then sit on the bucket, go to the bathroom, and cover your new creation in more kitty litter. Use a lot of kitty litter and completely cover your creation if you will be reusing the toilet and the same bag anytime soon. Otherwise, remove the bag, close it up, and set it aside in an airtight Ziploc freezer bag or other airtight container (along with previous creations) to toss into a dumpster or other outdoor trash receptacle later on when you get back to civilization.

Now do you see why I'm such a fan of using the facilities in town whenever possible?

You can buy plastic toilet seats made specifically to fit over the tops of 5-gallon buckets. A cheaper do-it-yourself alternative is to cut a piece of pool noodle or foam pipe insulation to the same length as the circumference of your bucket, cut a slit halfway though the noodle down its entire length, and place it around the rim of the bucket. Voila! A padded foam toilet seat!

A commercially available portable non-flush toilet is essentially a toilet seat with legs. You unfold the seat, set it on its legs, attach a plastic bag underneath the seat, and then proceed to use it in the same way as the bucket toilet. Online, at many Walmarts, and at many camping stores, you can buy leak-proof plastic

Figure 62. My folding collapsible toilet made out of PVC pipe and a toilet seat made to fit on a 5-gallon bucket

"Double Doodie" bags that are specifically made for this kind of portable toilet. They also work with the five-gallon bucket variety. These bags have liquid-absorbing and odor-masking gel in the bottom, making cleanup much easier. A box of six of these bags ranges from about $10 to $16.

I wasn't satisfied with any of the commercially available portable non-flush toilets. Most were far too big and bulky, and the ones that were smaller received poor reviews online because of durability issues. I decided that the best route for me was to design and make my own. I ordered one of the toilet seats that is made to fit on top of a 5-gallon bucket. Then I took 1-inch-diameter PVC pipe and made what is essentially a three-legged stool. I drilled a couple of holes in the seat and used cable ties through the holes to attach the seat to the PVC

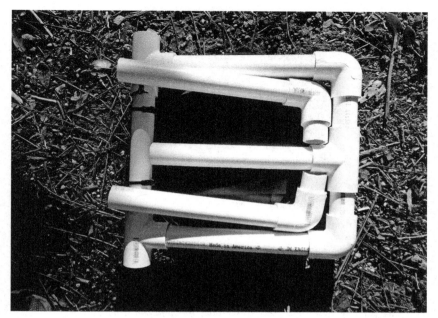

Figure 63. The portable toilet with its middle leg folded down and the two outside legs removed

frame. The legs are removable for compact storage. Figure 62 shows what it looks like when it's set up.

When I need to use the toilet, I lift up the toilet seat, grab a plastic bag, and put the top edges of the plastic bag around the PVC frame (I've omitted the bag from the photo for clarity) before lowering the lid seat on top of it.

One benefit of this kind of toilet over something like a bucket (apart from the much smaller amount of space it takes up, which is reason enough to use a design like this over any other) is that if I am out in the middle of nowhere in the desert or mountains, I can dig a hole, position the toilet over the hole, and do my business in it before covering it up. You can't do that with a bucket toilet. Figure 63 shows what it looks like when it's folded up and ready to be stored.

If you really wanted to, you could use a portable non-flush toilet inside of your SUV. This is not the best idea for what I think are pretty obvious reasons (smell being the main one), but it may be possible. A bucket toilet or other portable toilet similar in size could fit in on the floor between the front and rear seats if the seats were positioned far enough apart. (See Figure 64.)

One option if you are entertaining the possibility of going to the bathroom inside the vehicle is to use a bedpan. Because these aren't as tall as buckets, they could potentially be used when placed on a seat inside the SUV. I've never used one or even heard of anyone using one in an SUV, so I don't know how practical this actually is. You'd probably still want to use it with a plastic bag liner and kitty litter.

Figure 64. A bucket toilet positioned between the front and rear seats

Afraid of waking up in the middle of the night and needing to urinate? For guys, a wide-mouthed bottle with a secure screw-top lid works great, and I've read of women using wide-mouthed bottles, plastic food containers (like large yogurt or cottage cheese containers), and even Ziploc bags. These methods also work well when the weather outside is crummy and you simply don't want to leave your cozy confines.

Non-toilets

If you're out in the woods or desert, head a couple hundred feet away from a water source, dig a cathole at least 6 or 8 inches deep (a trowel or shovel is useful for this), squat over the hole, do your business, and cover it up. (See Figure 65.) Billions of people around the world use squat toilets everyday, but it takes some practice for those who haven't done it before. Put your used toilet paper in a Ziploc freezer bag and pack it back out to civilization and dispose of it there. I've been to far too many campsites with toilet paper sticking up out of the ground. An alternative is to burn it.

A variation of this if you can't or don't want to dig a hole is to lay out a few sheets of newspaper or a plastic bag or two, sprinkle some dirt, sawdust, or kitty litter (the last two brought specifically for this purpose) onto the newspaper/plastic bag, squat and do your business, sprinkle more kitty litter on top of your new creation, and then wrap the whole package up tightly and seal it in an airtight Ziploc bag for proper disposal later.

Portable toilets and privacy

If there is no natural barrier like bushes or boulders to give you some privacy while you do your business or shower, what are you going to do? If you can't find a suitable naturally occurring place, you might be able to use your SUV as a privacy wall. If you want to be sure you always have a private place, one option is to buy a portable privacy shelter. These are tall, skinny tents made specifically for privacy when changing clothes, showering, or going to the bathroom, and they start at around $25 online. The downside is that these are bulky when stored.

When I need privacy for showering or using a toilet, I simply use a tarp. The one I use is six feet (1.8 meters) long by nine feet (2.7 meters) wide. I use a very lightweight and packable tarp meant for ultralight backpacking (because I had it already), but any hardware store tarp would also work. Figure 66 shows my privacy tarp in action.

The tarp is folded down the middle so that it forms a V, and the open sides of the V go up against the side of the SUV. Both corners at the top of the tarp are attached to the roof of the vehicle (see the roof rack extender modification that I mention in Chapter 12, *Long-Term SUV RVing*). Two trekking poles are joined together to make one long pole (though any long pole can be used), and this pole is what keeps the tarp up. A paracord guy line is tied to the grommet at the top point of the V and wrapped tightly a few times around the top of the pole. The other end of the guy line is staked down to the ground a few feet away from the bottom point of the V. At the bottom edge of the tarp, another

Figure 65. The non-toilet alternative. A trowel (left) was used to dig a hole (center). A roll of toilet paper and a plastic bag for storing used toilet paper are to the right.

Figure 66. The privacy tarp in action. Note the hammer tied onto the bottom left corner of the tarp that can be lifted up to make entry to and exit from the privacy tarp possible.

stake goes through the grommet at the bottom point of the V, and another goes through one of the corner V grommets. The other bottom corner of the V has something heavy like a hammer or rock tied to it so that it can be lifted up to allow you easy entry and exit. Make sure people can't see through the vehicle's windows if that's something you care about.

The best thing about this setup is how small it packs down. The tarp packs down to the size of a one-liter water bottle. The pole that I use to keep the tarp up is actually two trekking poles (that I already have with me for when I hike) attached together to form a single longer pole. Apart from these few items, all I need are a few tent stakes and some paracord.

Keeping clean

Showering

As at home, the best way to keep clean on the road is to take a shower. Places with showers that SUV RVers can access include the following:

Campgrounds and RV parks – Many of the larger and more popular campgrounds have showers, as do most RV parks. Even if you're not spending the night at the RV park, try phoning ahead to see how much it costs to take a shower.

Public beaches with showers – These are great if they're in the area you'll be visiting, but using them is probably not ideal or even possible (they're often shut off) during the cooler months.

Truck stops – Among other services truck stops provide for truckers and RVers are showers. These usually cost around $10.

Hostels – Even if you aren't staying at a hostel (which may be worth it to shower, charge up electronics, and use the WiFi), you can often just go take a shower at one for a small fee, usually around $3 or $5. Call ahead to make sure.

Community swimming pools – Many community swimming pools also have showers. These are usually open only in summer and may require you to show a local ID.

Gyms – This is the best option for SUV RVers who will be spending a lot of time on the road and want a reliable place to take a shower. Membership to a nationwide chain (and I'm also including organizations like the YMCA here) is generally $30 to $50 a month plus any up-front setup fees. I signed up with one gym for several months but realized that my traveling style of using back roads and spending a lot of time in the mountains and desert didn't put me in the path of many gym locations. Other kinds of gym-like environments like climbing gyms and yoga studios may also have showers.

Swimming – If you want to get mostly clean, go for a swim in a nice lake, river, or other body of water. I recommend not using soap or shampoo because these can be harmful to local aquatic flora and fauna. Even biodegradable ones can be harmful.

Hotels, etc. – Getting a motel or hotel room is the nicest way to shower while on the road for an extended period of time, and it can even be economical if you don't indulge too often. I use Kayak.com (*http://kayak.com*), Booking.com (*http://booking.com*), and Hotels.com (*http://hotels.com*) to find the best rates at hotels. A cheaper alternative is to book a room in someone's house via a service like Airbnb (http://airbnb.com), something I've done many times all over the world and never had a problem with. CouchSurfing (http://couchsurfing.com) is similar to Airbnb but is free and often involves hanging out with the people who are hosting you (which can be both good and bad).

I know that many travelers use the showers in university gyms because these places rarely require you to show a school ID, but I'm not comfortable doing this since I'm not a student. I mention it because it may be something that works for you.

Powered portable showers

If you don't want to use any of the showers listed above, or if you'll be in places where such options aren't available, you can turn to portable showers.

These are generally not as convenient or comfortable as real showers, but they are an effective way to get clean and can be almost as good.

At the upper end of the camp shower spectrum is the heated camp shower. The heart of the heated camp shower is a water pump and a propane heater. The heater can be used with either a green one-pound propane canister or a larger twenty-pound tank. Using a heated camp shower requires a big bucket or jug of water (can be room temperature or even colder) into which you stick a water intake tube and a pump. Light the propane stove component, turn on the pump, and the water is pumped up through the heater element and through the shower tubing and out the showerhead. If the water is really cold, you can also recirculate it to get the temperature up to the point you'd like (i.e., the heated water coming out of the showerhead would just go straight back into the bucket or water container to be heated up again).

Similar to this is the water pump shower. The only difference here is that there is no heating element. You put one end that contains the battery-operated pump into the bucket of water, turn it on, and water comes out through the showerhead at the other end. If you want to shower with hot water, heat up a pot of water on a camp stove before putting it into the bucket.

Are you familiar with the hand-pressurized plastic chemical sprayers that gardeners, exterminators, lawn care specialists use? These can be converted into portable showers, and there are a few companies that sell ready-made showers of this type. You could also make your own. I did after finding an instructive how-to video online. (See Figure 67.)

I bought a two-gallon chemical sprayer, cut through the hose part near the sprayer head, and disposed of the sprayer head. Then I attached a kitchen sink sprayer head to one end of the new replacement hose and used a brass coupler to attach the other end of that hose to the hose connected to the sprayer unit. The total cost of the shower was about $30. To shower, I add water to the sprayer jug, pump

Figure 67. A portable pump shower made from a weed sprayer and replacement sink parts

up the handle a bunch of times (usually around 30), and spray away. I've found that a gallon of water is just about the right amount, and a gallon and a half is preferable if I'm particularly dirty. My showering process involves getting myself wet with the shower, turning it off and soaping up, and then using the shower again to rinse. To heat the water, I can either heat it up in a pot on my stove or set the water-filled jug out in the sun. A black trash bag around the jug helps the water inside heat up even faster in the sun.

This sprayer shower works great, and it actually almost feels like a real shower. I wish I'd made one of these when I first started traveling in my SUV. I even tried showering with the sprayer head that came with the sprayer unit before cutting it off and trashing it, and it worked pretty well. That particular sprayer head had three different settings: stream, cone, and fan. The stream and cone settings weren't practical for showering, but the fan one was.

Gravity showers

These showers involve some sort of large plastic or rubberized bag that you fill with water and hang from a tree or place atop your SUV. (See Figure 68.) A small tube with a showerhead at one end extends from the bag of water. The water can be heated either by leaving the bag out in the sun (including on top of your vehicle or on the dashboard while parked) or by heating it on a stove before pouring it into the bag. Gravity showers are relatively inexpensive, costing anywhere from $10 to $50.

One downside to the solar methods of heating water—and this applies to both the hand-pressurized plastic chemical sprayers and the gravity showers—is that you can't take a warm shower first thing in the morning because the sun hasn't been up long enough to warm the water. On the other hand, water that has been warmed by the sun during the day can provide you with a refreshing shower at the end of the day.

Before spending a lot of time camping in my SUV, I thought that a solar gravity shower was the perfect solution for me. They're cheap, very compact, and effective. What's not to like? The problem is that my style of

Figure 68. A solar shower hanging from an SUV

SUV RVing involves a lot of traveling—I'm always on the move and rarely in one space for long. Because I move around so much, I'd either forget to fill up the water bag and set it out to gather the sun's rays, or I wouldn't have time to set it up. Also, I found that having to hang the bag up was a bit of a pain. Still, I think that gravity showers are a great option if they fit your style of travel.

Dirtbag showers

The dirtbag shower is what I affectionately call a method of getting clean that can't accurately be described as a shower since you aren't standing under a real stream of water. The great thing about this type of bathing is that it can easily and discretely be done inside an SUV (although it's still easier to do outside). All it takes is a spray bottle and wet wipes (or wash cloth). Just spray yourself down with and then wipe yourself off. I've found that I can get myself relatively clean (or at least clean enough) using four wipes. I prefer wipes that have only a very small amount of very mild soap. The ones I use are biodegradable (although I still haul them out and properly dispose of them). They are made for camping and have very little odor. Try several different varieties and see which ones you like. If it's a sunny day, leave your spray bottle on the roof of your vehicle or on top of the dashboard under the windshield and the water will warm up relatively quickly. If you want to heat the water up even faster, put your reflective windshield sun shade up behind the bottle. (See Figure 69.)

If you want to wash your hair with shampoo, work a small amount into your wet hair and then wash it out using the spray bottle (you may want to put

Figure 69. A water bottle hanging in the front windshield with a reflective sun shade behind it

your head over a bucket or bin to collect the water if you're doing it inside your vehicle) and then dry your hair with a washcloth or towel.

Another way to clean your hair without a shower is to use dry shampoo. Dry shampoo is sprayed or dripped onto your hair. It absorbs the oil in your hair, and you then brush it out. While it's not a good substitute for complete rinses, it does work for occasional use when you're unable or unwilling to fully wash your hair. Again, try out a few different brands of the product to determine which one you like best. Talcum powder (baby powder) can also be used as an alternative in a pinch.

A cousin of the dirtbag shower is the hobo shower, which means washing up at a bathroom sink in a gas station, grocery store, or fast food restaurant. Because businesses typically frown on this kind of thing, I don't recommend it. If you are going to do it, try to find a smaller bathroom that you can lock, as it'll minimize the awkwardness for other people walking in while you're shaving or splashing water under your arms.

Miscellaneous shower thoughts and tips

One thing to keep in mind when using any of these bathing methods is how much water you have to use. It's easy especially with the battery-operated pump showers to go through a lot of water. Fill your water canister or bottle only with the amount of water you can afford to use.

If you're camping out in the middle of nowhere, it's probably not an issue to just shower naked next to your vehicle. If you want or need more privacy, use a privacy tent or tarp as described in the toilet section. If you want to shower in a semi-public area like a campground but don't have a private place to do so, wear a swimsuit.

To avoid getting your feet muddy while showering, either shower in flip flops (my preferred method; also a very good idea at truck stop, gym, and campground showers) or buy and stand on a doormat or shower mat (or one that has been cut in half). The problem with the latter method is that you'll then have to deal with a wet shower mat at the end of the shower, which may not be a big deal if you have the time to let it dry out before sticking it back in your vehicle. If possible, look for an area of rocky ground or other surface that won't get you too muddy.

And while this doesn't quite fall under the purview of showering, liberal use of hand sanitizer will keep your hands germ-free and feeling (and smelling) clean.

8. Electronics and Internet Access

To see additional relevant links for this chapter, visit
http://suvrving.com/book/eight/.

Not everyone is interested in using electronic devices while SUV RVing. I understand this. Indeed, the appeal of SUV RVing for some may be the opportunity to get away from phone rings and email pings. I am not going to judge your use or lack thereof of electronics but to offer those who do need or want to use their electronic devices guidance on the various ways to do so.

Powering electronic devices

There are multiple ways to power any kind of normal electric device while SUV RVing. If you can plug it into a wall outlet, you can figure out a way to have it in your SUV. Having said that, and before I get into the details of how to power or charge your devices, I want to simply mention that SUV RVing life is easier the fewer electronic things you have to worry about, run, or charge. Think very carefully and critically about the devices you have and how you use them before taking them with you. Are there analog tools you can use that will get the job done? Instead of taking notes on your phone, can you do it in a notebook? Instead of reading a book on your tablet, can you read a paper book? One example from my life is that I normally write in my journal every day (and have done so for years) on my laptop. When SUV RVing, however, I write my daily journal out by hand in a little binder because it saves on precious laptop battery life.

Alright, now let's move on to actually powering the devices.

Power inverters

For our purposes, a power inverter (usually shortened to just inverter) is something that you plug into your SUV's 12-volt power receptacle (i.e., the cigarette lighter) that lets you then charge or run your electronic devices. Inverters usually have 3-prong 110-volt AC outlets (i.e., wall outlets) and/or USB ports on them.

Figure 70. A small inverter with a USB cable and a two-pronged plug plugged in. The inverter sits in the SUV's cup holder.

It is important to understand the limits of these inverters, and to do that we need to talk about watts, amps, and volts. All inverters are rated to a certain wattage like, for example, 150 watts or 1,000 watts. This is the overall electrical load that the inverter can handle. Something like a microwave requires more wattage than a mobile phone. For reference, a small microwave needs about 1,000 watts to run, while my particular laptop needs about 45 watts. Charging a mobile phone requires 5 or 10 watts.

The wattage rating of the inverter you need would depend, of course, on your power needs. My inverter (Figure 70) is rated to 180 watts, meaning that I can charge or run multiple devices at a time as long as the total wattage requirements of those devices does not total more than 180. My inverter has one AC outlet and four USB ports, cost around $30, fits into a cup holder, and is great for my needs. I can charge my laptop (45 watts), my phone (5 watts), and a few external USB battery packs without any problem. If you don't know how many watts your electronics require, a simple online search will help tell you everything you need to know.

Watts are the product of two things: amps and volts. Amps are the amount or quantity of electricity that can pass though, and volts are the pressure or force of that electricity. If we think of amps and volts in terms of water running through a pipe, more amps equal a larger diameter pipe that can deliver more water (electricity), and more volts means that the water flowing through the pipe is at a higher pressure. Multiply amps by volts and you get watts.

Voltage is taken care of by the inverter and isn't really something we need to worry too much about. It takes the 12-volt DC current coming from the vehicle's battery and inverts it to 120-volt AC current for the inverter's three-pronged wall-type outlets. If the inverter has USB ports (the slots of the kind you'd find on a computer), it also takes that 12-volt DC power and steps it down to 5-volt DC power, which is what USB devices require.

But amperage *is* something we need to worry about, and it's dictated by the diameter or gauge of the wiring in your SUV (remember the pipe diameter analogy in the earlier paragraph). Even if I had an inverter rated to 2,000 watts and a microwave requiring 2,000 watts, I couldn't run a microwave because vehicle wiring isn't designed to deliver that much power (i.e., the microwave requires too many amps). Most vehicle power receptacles (i.e., cigarette lighter sockets) are connected to a 10-amp fuse (check the owner's manual of your SUV to see for sure), meaning that at anything over 10 amps, a fuse gets blown and you won't be able to use the power receptacle again until you replace the blown fuse. Were there no fuse in place, the wiring would continue to heat up, possibly to unsafe levels that could result in your vehicle catching fire. Multiple devices being charged by or getting power from the inverter at once draw more amps than a single device being charged at a time. In other words, more water needs to be carried by the pipe at a given time.

Because *Watts = Amps x Volts*, we also know that *Amps = Watts / Volts*. So if you've got a 2,000-watt microwave and it runs on 110 volts, we can divide 2,000 by 110 to get just over 18 amps. This would blow a vehicle's 10-amp fuse, and so you wouldn't be able to power that microwave from your vehicle's outlet.

All of this is to say that you will not be able to power certain items through your car's cigarette lighter socket (the power receptacle), even if you have a high-wattage inverter. If you do want to run high-wattage items like a microwave, air conditioner, or hair dryer, you'll need to attach them directly to high-capacity batteries that are properly wired for the task or get a generator.

It needs to be said that your vehicle's engine should be running when charging any electronics. Otherwise you could use up the charge in your vehicle's battery and have a dead battery when it comes time to start the vehicle. Whether your SUV's engine *needs* to be running in order to use the inverter to charge or run devices depends on your vehicle. The main 12-volt power socket in my SUV, for example, receives power only when the engine runs, but yours may also draw power when the engine is off. Charging a phone while driving reportedly[3] cuts fuel efficiency by 0.03 miles per gallon. If you're not driving anywhere, simply turn on the vehicle and idle the engine. Various estimates that I've read online[4] say that an idling automotive engine will burn between .2 and .5 gallons per hour, with more toward the upper end being burned if you're running the heater or air conditioner on full blast or charging multiple devices at once.

Some inverters are more efficient than others. A more efficient inverter uses slightly less of your battery's stored power than a less efficient inverter. The more efficient inverters are referred to as *pure sine wave* inverters and usually cost more than a less expensive and more common *modified sine wave* inverters (i.e., "normal" inverters). Pure sine wave inverters are also gentler on delicate electronics. That said, I personally feel that they are overkill for the needs of most SUV RVers who just need to run and charge basic items, where a normal inverter will work just fine.

House batteries

One way to power up all of your gadgets and gizmos is to have a house battery. (You could also chain multiple separate batteries together to form a higher-capacity house battery bank, but I will still refer to this simply as the house battery.) This is a battery that looks similar to an ordinary car battery, but you have it inside your SUV so you can plug all of your electricity-starved devices into it. It is distinct and separate from the starter battery that is under your SUV's hood. Like an ordinary vehicle battery, it is large and heavy. I don't know where the term house battery came from, but it's the general term used to describe the battery that runs auxiliary power in an RV or, in our case, an SUV RV. This includes powering lights and charging electronic devices. If you have a large-enough capacity house battery, you will also be able to power things like microwaves and refrigerators (assuming you have the appropriate inverter and wiring, as referred to above). If we go back to the water pipe example, the capacity of your house battery equates to the amount of water that's in the pond at the top of the pipe. You may have a wide enough pipe and enough pressure to run that microwave, but it won't do you any good if you're pumping water from a puddle (a low-capacity battery).

House batteries are deep-cycle batteries, often colloquially called marine batteries or golf cart batteries because boats and golf carts are two common uses for this type of battery. I am far from a battery wonk, so here is the definition of a deep-cycle battery per *Wikipedia*:

"A deep-cycle battery is a lead-acid battery designed to be regularly deeply discharged using most of its capacity. In contrast, starter batteries (e.g. most automotive batteries) are designed to deliver short, high-current bursts for cranking the engine, thus frequently discharging only a small part of their capacity. ... A deep-cycle battery is designed to discharge between 45% and 75% of its capacity, depending on the manufacturer and the construction of the battery. Although these batteries can be cycled down to 20% charge, the best lifespan versus cost method is to keep the average cycle at about 45% discharge. There is a direct correlation between the depth of discharge of the battery, and the number of charge and discharge cycles it can perform."[5]

So in other words, a deep-cycle battery is made to deliver a consistent amount of power down to roughly half or less (45–75%) of its stated capacity. You could run the battery down to 20% full before charging it back up again, but the battery will have a longer lifespan if it is kept above that. This capacity is measured in volts (the pressure in the pipe). You want to avoid having the voltage (pressure) drop too low.

How long will you be able to run a device on a given size of battery? Let's find out. The equation for finding amps that we covered earlier (*Amps = Watts / Volts*) also lets us know how long we can run a device on a given size of battery. Let's say we have a 100 aH (ampere-hour or amp-hour) battery. Because it's a deep cycle battery, we only want to use about half of its capacity (remember that we don't want to run it down much past that), so that gives us 50 aH to work with. And let's say we want to run a laptop in our SUV. What we need to do is figure out how many amps it will draw. To do that, we'll use our equation to solve for amps in *Amps = Watts / Volts*. My laptop draws 45 watts, so we divide that by 12 volts to get about 3.75 amps (45 / 12 = 3.75). That's how much of the battery's 100 aH capacity the laptop will use in an hour. So if we have 50 amp-hours to work with, and the laptop needs 3.75 amps per hour, we can theoretically run the laptop for just over 13 hours (50 / 3.75 = 13.33). Note that this does not take into account inefficiencies inherent to using a transformer, so the actual number of hours will likely be lower.

Before I continue on to discussing different house battery setups, I want to disclaim that this is not a primer on electrical systems. It is meant to give general background knowledge, and readers can do additional necessary research online to figure out how to build a system that meets their individual needs for powering various devices.

At a minimum, a practical house battery setup needs a couple of components, namely one or more batteries and an inverter. With this setup, you would initially charge the batteries at home using a wall-powered charge controller and then use them in your vehicle while you're on the road. Add a volt meter if you want to be able to monitor battery discharge. You can even buy commercial versions of this kind of setup marketed as solar generators. The "solar" part is a bit misleading, as you can still charge them from a wall outlet or your SUV's 12-volt power receptacle even if you don't have a solar panel.

One way to charge house batteries on the road is via the vehicle's alternator so that when the engine is running, the house battery is being charged. Search online for "charge auxiliary battery from alternator" and "van dwelling house battery alternator" (both without the quotes) to find schematics and other detailed information regarding these systems. This is a great setup that works well for a lot of vandwellers and RVers. The downside with this setup is that you'll need to drill holes in your vehicle to run the wiring from the alternator to the batteries and from the batteries to the vehicle frame for grounding purposes. This will make it a dealbreaker for many SUV RVers.

The other way to charge house batteries on the road is by using solar panels. In addition to the basic battery and inverter components, you'll need the solar panels themselves and a charge controller. A charge controller monitors and directs the amount of power coming in from the solar panels so that your batteries stay optimally charged and aren't damaged.

Solar panels can be packed inside an SUV during travel time and then set up outside and attached to the house battery at your campsite. Another option is to mount the solar panels on top of your SUV to harness solar power as you travel. However, if you want to have the house battery inside your SUV, you'd either have to drill a hole somewhere in the roof of your vehicle or run the wiring through a closed door or open window to connect the solar panels with the house battery. If you don't want to drill a hole in your SUV or have a wire permanently snaking down through a closed door or open window, you could have both the solar panels and batteries securely mounted on top of the vehicle, with the batteries being inside of a cargo box. Then, when power was needed you could simply run an extension cord down through an open window when at your campsite.

USB-powered devices

My SUV RV power system of choice doesn't have anything to do with large and heavy deep cycle batteries, complicated wiring, or solar panels, but it is great for nearly all of my needs and wants. I'm talking about USB power. USB-chargeable versions of nearly every conceivable electronic device can be found these days, including cameras, fans, headlamps, lanterns, speakers, camp showers, tablets, and even laptops. You can easily charge a USB device from a wall outlet (with a wall-to-USB adaptor that you can get for $5 or less), a computer, or an inverter that has USB ports on it.

What really make USB devices so great, in my opinion, are the external battery packs or power packs that you can buy. These are generally some sort of

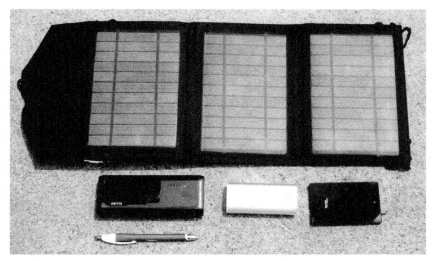

Figure 71. A folding solar panel with three external battery packs (and a pen for scale). A standard USB cable can connect the solar panel to any of these three external battery packs to charge them.

rectangular shape with rounded edges, and they range from the size of a credit card to the size of a hefty book. I have a couple of these battery packs of varying capacities that I use to charge the majority of my electronic devices. (See Figure 71.) By using an inverter that has USB ports, it's easy to charge these battery packs while driving. There are even USB battery packs large enough to charge a laptop a time or two.

I feel that USB power provides the best mix of all charging solutions for most SUV RVers. Their small size makes them easy to store and use while traveling. You can even buy portable solar panels to charge USB devices or the battery packs. Some devices like fans can run directly off of USB power, so you can plug the fan directly into the external battery pack that has been charging during your travel time.

The downside to USB power is that you won't be able to run microwaves, refrigerators, or other high-power devices from the battery packs. Still, I feel that a mixture of external USB-powered devices with external USB battery packs and an inverter that plugs into a power receptacle (cigarette lighter socket) along with an inverter is a great option for the majority of people on their short-term and even long-term SUV RV adventures. I like USB power so much that I now base purchases on whether or not an item can be charged via a USB connection. For example, I recently bought a new digital camera, and charging via USB cable was one essential feature I was looking for.

While we're talking about portable powered devices, remember that you can always simply use devices that run off of standard AA, AAA, C, or D batteries, both single-use and rechargeable. (Also know that you can charge these standard-sized rechargeable batteries via USB.) These are viable options for trips when you don't want to worry about having to take along equipment to charge devices or to have in an emergency in case the batteries in your USB-powered devices run down.

Finally, USB batteries can also be charged via solar panels. (See Figure 71.) There are several different portable solar panels on the market that have a USB port built-in, so to charge a USB battery pack or any device that can charge via USB, you simply need to plug it into the panel's USB port. No external charge controller or other wiring is needed.

Generators

Put gasoline into a generator, run it, and you get electricity out of it. This means that you can be camped out in the middle of nowhere, and as long as you've got gas in the tank, you can run all sorts of high-wattage items. A generator is handy not only for brief use of things like microwaves, blenders, and power tools, but it's also useful for topping up the charge in house batteries.

Because generators are loud and generally annoying to anyone around them, try not to run a generator for too long when you're in close proximity to other campers. In other words, don't use it to run a window air conditioning unit all night when you're in a crowded campground. (Many national parks have restrictions on generator use, and most RV parks have restrictions on the hours when you can use a generator. Additionally, hand-held motorized equipment, including generators, is generally prohibited in wilderness areas.) That said, modern generators made by companies like Yamaha and Honda are relatively quiet and don't take up too much space. The cheapest quiet ones currently sell for around $900. A louder generator on the cheaper end will cost about $120 to $150.

You probably won't want to store a generator inside your SUV unless you like the smell of gasoline, so you'll need to store it securely either on the roof of your vehicle or on a hitch cargo carrier. To figure out how long your generator will run on a gallon of gas, try it out before you leave home. Let it run on a gallon of gas until the it stops. That will be your gauge. Each generators is different.

Charging devices elsewhere

One important thing to keep in mind is that you can charge electronic devices in ways other than with your vehicle. The classic example is charging in a coffee shop, but this will also work in many other restaurants. Libraries and college campuses tend to have lots of wall outlets. Truck stops have chairs and tables with wall outlets nearby, as do highway rest stops and state welcome centers. If you're parked at a campsite that doesn't have power in a more developed campground, the campground bathroom might.

Useful electronic devices

So what electronic devices might you want to take with you on an SUV RVing trip? Here are some that I've found useful on trips ranging from just a couple of days to a month in length, though I don't take all of them on every trip:

- Lantern
- Headlamp
- Smartphone
- Laptop
- Digital camera
- Extra memory cards or hard drives
- Tablet and/or e-reader
- GPS unit – A handheld one for hiking and/or a dash-mounted one for driving.
- Portable speakers
- Headphones
- Portable WiFi hotspot
- Solar panels
- Battery packs
- Battery chargers

- Fans
- Thermometer/weather gauge
- Tripod and/or selfie stick – I know, these are not strictly electronic items, but close enough.

Other items that I personally don't use but that you might want or need include the following:

- Radar detector
- Microwave
- Refrigerator
- Blender
- Rice cooker
- Slow cooker (e.g., Crock-Pot)
- Satellite TV system
- TV
- Projector

Cable management

When I drive, I always have my phone sitting in its cradle on the dashboard. When I first started SUV Rving, it was always a pain to wrangle and untangle the phone's cables (charging cable and auxiliary audio cable) every time I needed to plug them back into the phone. I wanted to keep the cables more or less in place when they weren't being used so that they wouldn't mess with the gear shift lever. I finally ended up using a few very small adhesive-backed hooks to keep the cables in place. These are the hooks that you can easily remove by pulling a tab on the side of the adhesive part. The system works great. (See Figure 72.)

Figure 72. Two cables managed and held in place with small adhesive hooks

Figure 73. The hanging laptop desk

The hanging laptop desk

I work from my laptop, and I wanted to be able to use it while sitting in one of the front seats of the vehicle. After several design iterations, I eventually came up with the setup shown in Figure 73.

The platform under the laptop is made from plastic pegboard, though regular pegboard or any board with holes drilled into it would also work. I cut the platform to be just a bit larger than the footprint of my laptop. The rear end of the platform is tied onto the top of the steering wheel with short lengths of cord, and the front end is suspended with paracord from the solid points of the sun visor (though it could also be hung from adhesive hooks attached to the top of the windshield). It attaches and detaches quickly and stores away easily.

I use a wireless keyboard in my lap to type, and I set my road atlas on the center console and use that as a mouse pad and platform.

It pains me that I should even have to say this, but DO NOT USE a desk like this while driving! Only use it when parked!

If you don't want to make your own steering wheel laptop desk, there are some you can buy that are solid pieces of plastic that hook onto the steering wheel (search online for "steering wheel desk").

A cousin of the hanging laptop desk is the hanging phone holder, which I've found useful for I want to watch videos on my phone before going to sleep but don't want to tire out my arms by holding the phone up for two hours. I just stick my phone in a clear Ziploc bag, tie a piece of paracord across the interior of the SUV from one side to another, and use strong metal clips to attach the bag to the cord.

Useful smartphone apps

Because the app landscape is always changing and people prefer different mobile operating systems, I'm not going to recommend specific apps. Instead, here are general types of apps that you may find useful as an SUV RVer:

- Gas station locator apps
- Campground locator apps – I've found it helpful to have multiple campground locator apps because some include individual campgrounds or types of campgrounds that others don't.
- Restaurant and location review apps
- Data usage apps – Great for seeing how much of my monthly bandwidth allotment I have left.
- Camera apps – Some offer tools or settings that others don't. For example, I realized that I needed to be able to set the camera's timer for a minute or two to take certain kinds of pictures, and the built-in app didn't offer that functionality. I eventually found one that let me set the length of the timer.
- Photo processing apps
- Messaging apps
- Social apps
- Email apps
- Audio apps for music, audiobooks, podcasts, etc.
- Reading apps
- Map apps – Apps in which you can download the maps offline occasionally come in very handy.
- Video and audio recording apps
- Read-it-later apps – These let you add online articles to a queue that your phone downloads for offline reading.
- Weather apps
- Free WiFi locator apps
- Restroom locator apps
- VPN (virtual private network) apps – More on these in the *Internet access* section below.
- Shopping apps
- Entertainment apps (e.g., Netflix, etc.)

Internet access

There are two main ways to get internet access while on the road: WiFi and mobile networks. WiFi is free in many places, including libraries, restaurants, coffee shops, truck stops, stores, gyms (if you're a member), laundromats, and even parks and rest areas. If the location is part of a well-known national chain, there's a good chance that it has free WiFi. Most of these places don't require a password, but you may need to check a box in your web browser saying that you agree to their terms before getting online.

My personal favorite places to score free WiFi are libraries (call ahead or look on the library's website to see whether a local library card is needed; it rarely is) and McDonald's restaurants. If the library WiFi is password-protected, the password is usually posted somewhere. I've seen it on the door to the library, on a piece of paper near the computer workstation areas, and on the library's website.

The sandwich chain Subway usually doesn't have the fastest or most reliable WiFi, but there are Subways absolutely everywhere, so they're a good backup to know about. If you want to sit in your vehicle to access the free WiFi, park in front of a Dunkin Donuts, McDonald's, or Starbucks. If you want to be able to park a bit further away from these and other places but still get a strong WiFi signal, consider purchasing an antenna/signal booster that plugs into your laptop.

If you're in a larger city and would like a place where you can access fast internet, have the option to print, rent a conference room, or be in an environment with other professionals, consider visiting a coworking space. Some of these require monthly membership fees, but many are flexible and offer daily usage options, punch-card visits (e.g., ten visits in a month-long period), and weekly memberships.

If using open-access WiFi, you might want to use a VPN (virtual private network). This is a way to safeguard your connection to the network. It encrypts the data flowing to and from your computer or mobile device to make sure no one else can read it. This is especially useful when entering sensitive information like credit card numbers and passwords. Places like libraries that have strict internet filters may also block VPNs.

Most of us these days can access the internet on our smartphones and tablets, though this obviously won't be possible if you are out of range of the cellular network. (Side note: I've never found the carrier maps of network coverage to be very accurate, so don't rely on them for trip planning.) If your mobile plan allows you to tether (not all do), you'll be able to access the internet on a laptop or other devices through your tethering-enabled phone or tablet.

Another way to get online is via a mobile hotspot. This is a small rectangular or square-ish device that uses cellular data to create a WiFi network that phones, tablets, and computers can then connect to. It essentially does what a tethering-enabled phone can do, but it's done without the phone or tablet. While some mobile hotspots require monthly plans, others are pay-as-you-go, making them more appropriate for people like SUV RVers who may need mobile internet connectivity for only a certain length of time.

If you have multiple mobile network-connected devices and will be doing a lot of SUV RVing, it's not a bad idea to have plans with two different carriers. This increases your chance of getting a signal wherever you are. I have one carrier for my phone and another for my mobile hotspot, and there have been several times when I've been able to get online with one but not the other.

Satellite internet is also an option if you really want to get online when you're out in the boonies, but it is slow, expensive, and unreliable, plus it requires bulky and expensive equipment.

However you access the internet, I recommend monitoring your WiFi and data usage to see how much you actually use and what your bandwidth requirements are. Most cellular network data providers will provide this information in your account, but you can get more specific detailed data by installing a data usage app. These apps can also monitor WiFi usage. There are also bandwidth monitoring apps for the major desktop operating systems. Monitoring is a great way to understand how much bandwidth steaming or downloading video and audio uses up so you will know if you are about to go over your data limit while on the road.

9. Keeping the SUV Clean

To see additional relevant links for this chapter, visit http://suvrving.com/book/nine/.

The outside

I don't really have too much to say about keeping the outside of an SUV clean. I wash my vehicle whenever I think it gets too dirty. It's not rocket science. I will say that my vehicle gets dirtier faster when I'm out adventuring in it, so SUV RVing means that I wash it more often than I otherwise would. Apart from that, there are a few other little things I want to mention.

First, when you've stopped to fill up your vehicle with gas, you should take the time to wash the windshield and rear window with the squeegee and cleaning fluid at the pump. This will ensure that there is at least a modicum of visibility. If there's any part of your vehicle that should be clean, it's the windows.

Second, if you're camping in the mountains and are parked under pine trees, you may find that pine sap has dripped onto your vehicle. After leaving my SUV in a Yosemite National Park parking lot for two weeks while I hiked, it was absolutely covered in pine sap drippings. Not great. Scrubbing it with a wet rag didn't have any effect, but wiping it with a rag dipped in rubbing alcohol worked wonderfully.

Finally, I've found that coin-operated, self-service car washes work great and are inexpensive (as cheap as a couple of dollars). I use them often, but I take my SUV in to a full-service car wash facility to get a more detailed and expensive wash and vacuum after a long trip. I've heard of some people using the self-service washes to shower (i.e., wash themselves). I don't recommend this. You'll look like a crazy person, and the force of the water coming out of the spray is such that it can actually cut through your skin. I've heard of it happening.

The inside

Mats, covers, etc.

There's a lot more to keeping the inside of your SUV clean than the outside. Let's start with the floor. I have aftermarket floor mats. I have one for each front

Figure 74. A rubber floor mat with internal ridges that keep liquids from spreading

seat and two for the rear bench seat. I bought a set of rubber floor mats made specifically for my year, make, and model of SUV, so they fit perfectly. (See Figure 74.) They were more expensive than more generic ones I could have bought, but I feel they were worth it. Because I knew that I would be traipsing through wet, muddy, and occasionally snowy areas, I went with the waterproof rubber mats instead of fabric ones. Whenever they get too gross for my liking, I just have to hose them down at home or rinse them off at the self-service car wash. If you're shopping for floor mats, try to get ones with ridges and edges that keep any trapped water or grime from spilling over elsewhere.

I also bought a fitted plastic mat made specifically for my SUV's rear cargo area. This keeps the carpet back there clean and in good shape. An unforeseen bonus is that the slick surface makes it easier to load and unload the heavy plastic bin that I store in the back. If you don't want to buy a cargo area mat, you could make your own out of carpet, wood, or bamboo mats. Office chair floor mats are another possibility. They might not fit the back of your specific vehicle perfectly, but they are easily found at any office supply store and could be trimmed to fit your SUV.

If parts of your body other than your feet will be getting wet, muddy, or snowy, invest in seat covers. Universal seat covers are inexpensive and can be put on and taken off easily. They may not fit as snugly or be as aesthetically appealing as your original seat covers, but they will get the job done.

I installed a steering wheel cover on my steering wheel both to protect the wheel from wear and to give a bit of cushion and insulation on those frigid mornings.

Cleanliness

The easiest way to keep your SUV clean is simply to not let anything dirty or messy inside. Kick your shoes together to knock any loose gunk off before you step into your vehicle. Leave your shoes outside if you'll be inside for a while. Use your camp shower to clean off sandy or dirty items.

The second easiest way to keep your SUV clean is to segregate the dirty or messy items. Put those sandy shoes into a plastic bag. Put a tarp under the muddy cooler before you set it on that seat. Use a plate or paper towel under that slice of pizza. In fact, try not to eat inside your vehicle at all, and if you do, quickly wipe up any crumbs or messes that result.

I like to keep a roll of paper towels on hand at all times inside my vehicle. Feeding a bungee cord through the middle of the paper towel roll and then hanging it from the back of the passenger side headrest supports is a great way to keep the paper towels out of the way yet accessible. (See Figure 75.)

The reality is that no matter how fastidious you are about keeping the inside of your SUV clean, it'll get dirty. Either vacuum it out at home between trips, vacuum it out yourself at a do-it-yourself car wash while you're on the road, take it in to get it vacuumed at a car wash, or travel with a small 12-volt auto vacuum.

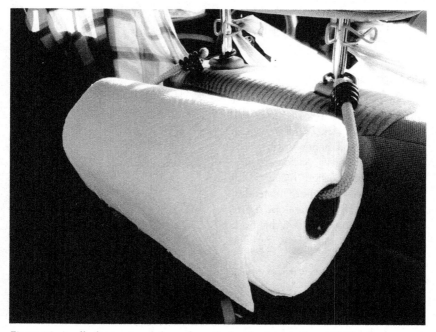

Figure 75. A roll of paper towels hung from the headrest support posts with a bungee cord

Related to keeping the SUV clean is keeping everything inside of it tidy. The tidier your space is, the easier it will be to find things and the more appealing the interior of your SUV will be. The three pillars of SUV tidiness are as follows:

1. The fewer things you have, the easier it is to keep the SUV tidy.
2. Find a home for everything and always put everything back in its home after using it.
3. Organizing aids (e.g., pockets, bins, drawers, nets, etc.) can help you keep things organized, but having too many of these things will still create clutter.

The inside of your vehicle will eventually become dusty, especially if you drive a lot on dirt roads. Using an automotive cleaner like Armor All (which also comes in wet wipe form) will keep things looking nice and clean. If you need to clean some hard-to-reach places, get canned air (the cans of compressed gas used to clean computer keyboards) and go to town.

The reality of spending a lot of time in a small confined space is that it can start to smell bad. Good practices here are to remove trash often, keep dirty clothes packed away, avoid eating and cooking inside the vehicle, wash your clothing and bedding materials regularly, and minimize condensation by having adequate ventilation. Air fresheners can help mask unpleasant odors. I also have a small bottle of Fabreeze that I'll occasionally spray the interior of the vehicle with. When you're not inside your SUV, keeping the windows rolled down an inch or two helps the vehicle air out.

Dealing with trash

The biggest issue for me when it comes to keeping the inside of my SUV clean is trash. Food wrappers, used tissues and paper towels, brochures, maps, leaves, packaging, disposable water bottles, receipts—all of it has to go somewhere. Instead of just tossing it all onto the floor, figure out a waste disposal system that both works for you and keeps garbage sprawl to a minimum.

I like to use plastic grocery bags as trash bags. They're free, strong, and don't take up much space when stored. I keep about twenty of them stuffed tightly into a small drawstring

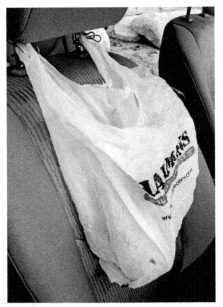

Figure 76. A grocery bag used as a trash bag. It is clipped to the front of the passenger seat headrest posts.

Figure 77. The folder in the front passenger side door slot used to store maps, brochures, etc.

stuff sack. I call it my grocery bag sausage, and I add bags to it whenever I get them. When I need a new trash bag, I withdraw one from the sausage and clip it to the front passenger seat headrest posts. (See Figure 76.)

I've found that one of these can hold about three days worth of my trash on average (though I may dispose of it sooner depending on the odors). When it's time to get rid of the trash bag, I remove the bag from the clips, tie up the bag, and throw the bag away at someplace like a grocery store or gas station. If I'm disposing of empty soup cans, I'll put the cans into a Ziploc bag so that they won't leak out into the trash bag and onto my seats. A rule of thumb I use is that if the item could somehow potentially stain or otherwise mess up my seats, I put it in a Ziploc bag before placing it in my trash bag.

Because I like to visit national parks and monuments, I end up with a ton of brochures, newsletters, and maps. I put these into a plastic folder that fits perfectly in the little storage slot on the passenger side door. (See Figure 77.) Having them all there in the folder makes removing them much easier. If you want to keep these around for informational purposes, consider taking photos of the pages that interest you and tossing the rest.

10. What to See and Do

To see additional relevant links for this chapter, visit
http://suvrving.com/book/ten/.

It can be hard to keep track of all of the things you want to see or places you want to visit on a trip and make sure you see them in the right order to avoid backtracking or wasted time and gas. I've found that printing off the map of a state or region onto a single piece of paper helps. Then I mark all the spots I want to visit. This gives me a good overview and helps me plan my route better.

What to see

Where you should go and what you should see in your SUV depends on, among other things, where you live, what your budget is, what you like to see and do, how much time you have, what season it is, what the weather is like, and what your interests are. It's impossible to give blanket advice on things to see that will apply to everyone reading this, but some places that you might want to add to your itinerary include the following:

National parks – If I could do nothing but explore the national parks for the rest of my life, I would die a happy man. These are the number one item on my list of things to see and do, and I make it a point to visit national parks whenever possible. Yes, they can be crowded during the high season (usually summer, except for some of the desert parks like Death Valley and Big Bend), but even then the parks are so large and visitation so concentrated that it's possible to find a spot you can have all to yourself. Buy an annual national parks pass (which is also good for entry into national monuments and other federal fee areas) and explore to your heart's content. If you are at least 62 years old and a United States citizen or permanent resident, you can buy a lifetime Senior Pass at a sharply discounted rate. Active US military personnel can get an annual national parks pass for free.

National monuments – I think of national monuments as proto-national parks or national parks in embryo. Indeed, many national parks were national monuments before being upgraded to national park status. What you find in national monuments is often every bit as spectacular as what you find in national parks, but national monuments tend to be smaller. Instead of a national park's many scenic wonders, a national monument might include just one or a small handful of standout features. National monuments are sometimes less developed than national parks in terms of things like visitor centers, restaurants, and other amenities.

State parks – State parks are hit or miss for me. Some showcase features, formations, and landscapes worthy of any national park. Others (I'm thinking of those that are essentially just a lake or reservoir) are rather unremarkable. A quick online image search of a park that you've seen on a map or read about is a fast and easy way to see whether that park is a hit or miss for you.

Natural attractions – While driving on back roads in western Utah, I saw a sign that pointed to a "Great Stone Face" a few miles down a dirt road. Intrigued, I turned and followed the road to a natural stone outcropping that, when viewed from a certain angle, indeed looked like a face in profile. I love stuff like this. Also included in this category of natural attractions are scenic waterfalls, trees, lakes, canyons, beaches, cliffs, mountains, and viewpoints.

Scenic drives – There are 150 National Scenic Byways and All-American Roads[6] in the United States. These are roads singled out for their scenic beauty or other outstanding qualities. I love a good drive, and I've found that going out of my way to drive these roads and others found through online searches (e.g., "scenic drives Arizona") and books (there are books dedicated to scenic drives for many of the states) is always worth the detour.

Historical sites – I'm a history nut. If it's old and has a neat story, I'd like to see it. I'll stop for interesting towns, markers, ruins, battlefields, art, and monuments. If you want to see some historical greatest hits, seek out National Historic Landmarks in the places you'll be visiting.

Amusement parks – Love roller coasters? Want to cool off at a water park? Find the best amusement parks along your intended travel route and get your fix.

Museums – Art museums, history museums, living museums, sculpture gardens, interpretation centers, wax museums, halls of fame, children's museums, dinosaur museums—there are enough museums out there for any interest. Even if you're on a budget, there are enough free museums (and museums with occasional free days) to still keep you busy.

Hot springs – Hot springs are relaxing and often scenic places to unwind and relax after a long drive or hike. Check out Soak.net (*http://soak.net*) for a hot spring database and seek out hot spring-specific guidebooks for the region or state you'll be exploring.

Factory tours – Many companies open up their production facilities to the public through factory tours. I went to the Jelly Belly candy factory north of

San Francisco and had a great time learning about how jelly beans are made and getting some free samples. Some factory tours are free and others charge a fee. Some may also require reservations, so be sure to plan ahead. A great resource for finding factory tours is Factory Tours USA (http://www.factorytoursusa.com/).

Fairs, festivals, and holidays – There are all sorts of celebrations going on all over the country on a given day, and being an SUV RVer gives you a great chance to take part in them. They run the gamut from Shakespearean poetry festivals to road kill cook-offs. If you really love this type of thing, there are entire books dedicated to the subject that will give you enough road trip fodder for years.

Roadside attractions – I love seeing things that I've never seen before, and roadside attractions are a great way for me to get my fill of oddities. From giant pineapples in people's front yards to funky art in the middle of nowhere, there's something strange out there for everyone. Roadside America (*http://www.roadsideamerica.com/*) is the definitive resource for these lovable oddities.

Notable restaurants – Visiting restaurants and diners is a great way to understand the local culture better and to try new things. You can also simply visit ethnic food restaurants for cuisines that you've never tried before, or pay special visits to restaurants that you've heard about, have seen seen on TV, or that have received awards.

Figure 78. An old cemetery in the ghost town of Terlingua, Texas, just outside of Big Bend National Park

Cemeteries – I've been told that I'm weird for loving to visit cemeteries, but there must be others out there like me. I love looking at the different headstones, reading the different names, and enjoying the peace and quiet. It's also fun to see which famous people are buried in the cemeteries of the towns you'll be passing through. Find a Grave (*http://www.findagrave.com/*) is a great resource for this. (See Figure 78.)

Stores – If you love to shop, collect, or browse, make these a priority while traveling. Even if you don't love to shop, you might want to see if there's anything you can get on the road that isn't available in your hometown.

Special interest locations – Try to cater your travels and adventures to the things you're interested in. I love to rock climb, so I often try to fit rock climbing areas into my travels. Into spooky stuff? Find purportedly haunted places to visit. Love baseball? Get tickets to stadiums you've never been to.

Meetups – If you want to meet new people who share your same interests, search for meetups (*http://meetup.com*) in your destination area. Having a simple business card or name card with your name, blog URL, email address, and/or other contact information is a great way to stay connected with people you meet at meetups or elsewhere on the road. My business card simply has the URL of my personal website, which has contact information and links to social media profiles

Local events – If you know you'll be in a certain city or town on a certain date, go online and search for "[city name] events calendar." My girlfriend and I do this a lot, and as a result we've seen and done great things that we otherwise would have missed entirely. A couple of our favorites have been a chocolate festival and a bagpipe band performance.

Resources

So how exactly do you find some of these interesting places to see? Other than the previously mentioned websites, here are some additional resources:

- Guidebooks
- Online searches (e.g., "things to see in New Orleans" or "Denver museums" or "off the beaten path Miami")
- TripAdvisor (*http://tripadvisor.com*) – A site with crowdsourced ratings of attractions and restaurants.
- Yelp (*http://yelp.com*) and UrbanSpoon (*http://urbanspoon.com*) – The homes of crowdsourced restaurant ratings.
- Travel blogs
- Atlas Obscura (*http://atlasobscura.com*) – A website dedicated to unusual things all around the world.

- Friends and family – Tell people where you're going and see if they have any recommendations.
- Experts – Ask the people who know best. I always try to ask park rangers in national and state parks what their favorite part of the park is. Be sure to ask the locals you meet about the area's highlights.

Hobbies

Hobbies that require a minimal amount of "stuff" are ideal for SUV RVers, and these include the following:

- Games – A great way to have fun, enjoy the company of your traveling companions, and meet new people. Card games, dice games, and mobile phone or tablet games are especially well suited to SUV RVing.
- Reading – Ebooks take up much less space.
- Playing a small musical instrument
- Listening to music
- Drawing/sketching/painting
- Writing
- Photography
- Creating videos
- Whittling
- Knitting/cross-stitch/crocheting
- Blogging – A great way to document your travels, share them with others, and potentially meet new people.
- Hiking
- Camping (obviously)
- Shooting – Guns, BB guns, slingshots, bows and arrows, etc. Make sure the weapon is legal in the states you'll be visiting.
- Running
- Walking
- Swimming
- Dancing
- Disc golf
- Geocaching
- Badminton
- Ball sports
- Horseshoes and other yard games
- Volunteering
- Bird watching
- Animal track or sign identification
- Journaling
- Foreign language study
- Juggling

- Metal detecting
- Panning for gold
- Attending local events
- Watching movies or TV shows
- Sudoku and crossword puzzles
- Astronomy
- Video games
- Podcasts and audiobooks – Great to listen to on those long drives.

Also, keep in mind that the equipment for many outdoor activities and hobbies (e.g., skiing, kayaking, bicycling) can often be rented, so you don't necessarily need to take it with you.

11. Safety and Security

To see additional relevant links for this chapter, visit http://suvrving.com/book/eleven/.

Safety is important everywhere, but at first glance it might seem like there are a lot more opportunities for harm or injury to come to those SUV RVing. You're in a new, unfamiliar area, you're putting yourself in situations that you may not normally put yourself in, and you're potentially more exposed and vulnerable. The best way to stay safe while SUV RVing is to be aware of your surroundings. Drive through a potential camping or sleeping area and make sure it seems safe before deciding to spend the night there. Know who is around you. Avoid areas of high crime. Trust your gut and don't stay in a place that you have bad feelings about. When staying the night in an urban or suburban area, try to make your vehicle look as inconspicuous as possible. Keep your mobile phone charged and within reach, and be aware of when you don't have reception. Always know where your keys are.

When parking your vehicle for the evening, back into your site and keep your vehicle keys within reach while sleeping. If during the night there is any question of the intentions of someone or something outside your vehicle, you can then immediately get into the driver's seat and easily leave the area. Every day before you start driving, walk around your vehicle and visually inspect everything. How do the tire treads and sidewalls look? How's the air pressure in the tires? Are all of the doors and windows closed? If you have things strapped or anchored somewhere on the outside of the vehicle, are they securely attached? Do all of the lights work? Did you leave anything on top of the vehicle or on the ground? Is your vehicle leaking important fluids? Is there anything you need to watch out for when you drive out of your campsite?

My mom told me recently about a terrifying incident that happened to one of her friends. After loading her kids into her SUV, she set off down the road at about 40 miles per hour. Suddenly one of the vehicle's front wheels flew off, and the SUV was totaled in a one-car crash. Thankfully no one was injured. The investigating police officers concluded that the wheel had been missing a few lug nuts. It's likely that someone had been in the process of stealing the wheel off the SUV but had not removed all of the lug nuts before leaving or being scared off. The driver hadn't noticed that one of her front wheels had most of the lug nuts missing. This is the kind of thing that could be avoided by a pre-drive inspection.

Getting stuck or stranded

One of my biggest fears is that something terribly wrong will happen to my vehicle to render it immovable while out in the middle of the desert or up in the mountains. It has, in fact, happened to me, though it was before I had my SUV. I was out in Utah's West Desert to climb an obscure mountain. The West Desert is incredibly remote. Very few people live out there, and there are no services (including cellular service). To say that it is the middle of nowhere is an understatement.

Getting to the base of the mountain required driving on a dirt road for a couple of hours. I made it out there just fine and successfully made my way up and down the mountain. Disaster struck on the way back, however. I had driven the car only a few hundred yards down the dirt road from the trailhead when I got the worst flat tire I've ever seen. The wheel wasn't punctured by a rock as much as it was viciously slashed by one. I needed a new tire. I had a spare, so I retrieved it, got out the jack, jacked up the car, and removed the wheel. While the damaged wheel was off but before I was able to put the spare on, the weight of the car shifted on the soft, sandy road and it fell to the ground, bending the small jack and rendering it unusable as it did so.

I was in trouble. I was in the middle of nowhere, my car was on the ground and missing a wheel, and I had no way to get the car back up off the ground to put it back on. I had seen a lone house a couple of miles back down the road when I was driving into the area (always be aware of such things), and I decided that my only hope was to make my way there on foot and see if anyone could help me. I made the trek and approached the house with caution. I knew that if people lived way out in the boonies like this, there was a good chance that they didn't want to be disturbed. It was getting to be later in the afternoon, and no lights were on in the house. A couple of skinny peacocks roamed the yard and eyed me warily. The place just felt creepy. I knocked on the door and waited but heard nothing. I knocked again, and again there was no response. Defeated, I headed back to the car.

It was nearly dark at this point, and I knew I'd have to spend the night in my car. I'd planned this to be a day trip, not an overnight or multi-day excursion, so I didn't have a sleeping bag or blanket. It was early summer in the desert and the day had been hot, but the high elevation of the area promised and delivered a cool night. I had the clothes that I was wearing and an extra jacket to keep me from freezing. Luckily I'd had the foresight to stock the car with plenty of food and water for the trip, so I wasn't in any immediate danger.

I leaned the passenger seat back as far as it would go and bent my legs so that I could put them up on the dashboard. The night was long, cold, and uncomfortable, but I made it through unscathed. Once it was light enough to see,

I traipsed back to the main dirt road in the area and sat down to wait for a passing car that I could flag down and get some help from. I waited for two hours and didn't see a soul. Dispirited, I decided to once again try the creepy farmhouse nearby. It was much less creepy in the bright light of the morning, and my knock on the door was soon answered by an older woman. She looked at me suspiciously, and after I'd explained my situation, she pointed to a large building nearby and said, "They're in the barn," before shutting the door. I approached the barn and looked in to see an elderly man and a younger man in his early twenties working on a car. I later found out they were grandfather and grandson.

They listened to my tale and sprang into action, grabbing an enormous pneumatic jack and hopping into a pickup truck, indicating that I should join them. We rode up to my poor, disabled little car, jacked it up off the ground, and installed the donut spare tire. The older man was unimpressed with my spare, saying that I'd never make it back out to civilization again with that thing on. He told me to follow him back to the house, which I did. He took me out back behind the barn and showed me a pile of worn but still usable tires. We found one that would fit my car, and he loaded it and my wheel rim onto a fancy contraption of some sort that mated the two together. I thanked the man profusely for his help and tried to give him some money for the tire and the help, but he refused. I managed to slip it to his grandson instead.

I drove very, very slowly and carefully over the mountains to a small town in Nevada, where I was able to get a proper new tire for the drive back home.

There are a few morals to the story here. First, it's a good idea to tell people where you're going whenever you're heading out into more remote areas. If I hadn't returned after a few days, the people I'd alerted could have sent a search party out to find me. Second, only travel to areas that your vehicle can handle safely. I was over my head on those rough, remote roads in my little Plymouth Breeze. Third, I recommend being able to get yourself out of any situation you're likely to encounter. Have an escape plan for the worst case scenario. What will you do if you get stuck somewhere remote and can't call for help? Fourth, always have emergency food, water, and warm clothing in your vehicle just in case something does go wrong. Fifth and finally, don't judge a book by its cover. The ghetto, scary farmhouse turned out to house mercifully kind and helpful people. Who knows how long I would have had to wait on that dirt road for a vehicle to pass by?

A membership with AAA ("Triple A"—the Automobile Association of America) is something that all SUV RVers should consider. Membership benefits vary depending on the plan but include towing, flat tire repair or replacement, battery jump-starting and replacement, emergency fuel delivery, and lockout/locksmith services. Even if you don't end up using the services, knowing that you have them gives peace of mind. It's worth noting that AAA will not tow you if you're on a dirt road, so bear that in mind when planning out your adventures. You'll be on your own out there.

Getting stuck in sand, mud, or snow is a big fear of mine. A winch could provide big peace of mind. Other than that, what a stuck vehicle really needs is traction, so what you want to do is give the wheels something they can bite into to get more traction. This can be in the form of rocks, dirt, floor mats, newspapers, clothes, cardboard, carpet scraps, or blankets. Take those things and place them in front of the powered drive wheels. You can even buy mats or pads made specifically for placing under your tires to provide traction. Chains are also an obvious option here and necessary if you will be traveling a lot through snowy areas. A small folding shovel can be handy for clearing snow or mud away from the tires and for digging a clear path for your tires to take. Some people who travel a lot in snowy areas have sand or kitty litter in their vehicle that they can use to sprinkle on the snow to provide more traction for the tires.

Weapons

I think that the vast majority of people out there are good and that the odds of a bad person doing anything to you are infinitesimally small. I do not carry a gun or other serious weapon in my SUV, though many people do. That's their choice and right. If you do want to have a gun in your vehicle, be sure to check the laws in your state and the states you'll be traveling through regarding the concealment and transportation of firearms.

In addition to a few knives that I have in my SUV (more for practical use than defensive purposes), I do have a small can of pepper spray, though I'm not quite sure in what situations it would be useful. Still, it provides me with some comfort. Bear spray might make sense if you frequent bear country. Note that pepper spray and bear spray should not be left in a vehicle in hot weather. The canisters cannot tolerate the high temperatures of the inside of a vehicle in hot weather and will explode if they get too hot. If a can of pepper spray or bear spray explodes in a vehicle, the interior will be impregnated with the spray and it will be impossible to be inside the vehicle for several weeks, if not several months.

A tire iron or baseball bat could also be used to fend off attackers in a pinch.

Emergencies

Even though I'm no mechanic, doctor, or survival expert, there are several things that I currently carry in my SUV (or am looking to buy in the near future) to give myself an extra margin of safety and a feeling of security. (See Figure 79.) The items include the following:

- Spare tire and jack (and the knowledge of how to use them!)
- Road flares
- Reflective vest
- Tire pressure gauge

- Air compressor
- Fix-A-Flat or similar tire hole sealer
- Jumper cables
- Emergency portable jump starter
- Basic tools: hammer, wrenches, pliers, box knife, duct tape – Even if you don't know how to use them to fix something on your vehicle, someone who does might come along and be able to help you. My dad likes to tell the story of when he was driving a VW van on a very remote mountain road in Taiwan in the 1960s when he suddenly came across a car that had broken down due to a broken rubber hose. All he had on hand was masking tape, but he was able to apply it "more than liberally" (his words) to the hole. With some additional water in its radiator, the car was able to limp back to civilization.
- Vehicle manual
- Flashlight
- Matches, lighter, or other fire-starting method
- First aid kit
- Emergency money
- Hidden spare key
- Small fire extinguisher
- GPS unit
- Carbon monoxide detector
- Smoke alarm
- Small shovel
- Work gloves

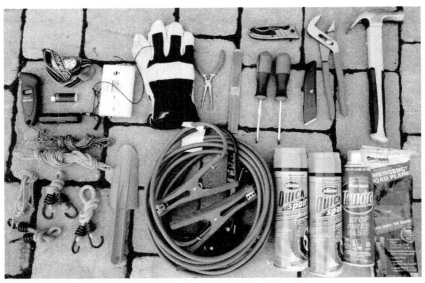

Figure 79. Some of the emergency items and tools I keep in my SUV

Weather

Extreme weather can turn a pleasant and routine day of SUV RVing into an extremely unpleasant or dangerous one. Know what the upcoming weather conditions are by checking the forecast regularly, and make sure you've got appropriate emergency items in your vehicle. A portable weather radio can also be useful.

Here are some ways to deal with various forms of extreme weather:

Extreme heat – Use a windshield sun shade when your SUV is parked. Park in the shade. Make sure your air conditioner is working. Have plenty of water in your vehicle. Take portable battery-powered fans with you.

Extreme cold – Insulate any water bottles or jugs to keep them from freezing, or keep any smaller bottles under the covers with you when you sleep. Have adequate insulation for yourself in the form of jackets, blankets, sleeping bags, etc. A reflective emergency blanket is also a good thing to have.

Extreme rain – Confirm that your windshield wipers are in good shape and can effectively clear the windshield. Move to higher ground, and do not try to ford streams or roads that have become waterways. If you drive a lot in rainy conditions, consider applying Rain-X or another spray-on water repellant to your vehicle's windshield. Stash an emergency poncho somewhere in your SUV. Umbrellas are handy for moderately rainy conditions, especially in warmer weather where wearing a jacket or poncho would cause you to sweat and get wet anyway.

Extreme snow – Wear insulated, waterproof footwear. Use all-season tires, snow tires, or chains. If the snow is heavy, pull into a parking lot, wait for the worst of the storm to pass, and consider getting a hotel room. Have a good snow brush and scraper. Have tools and materials that will help you out of the snow if you get stuck.

Extreme bugs – While technically not extreme weather, extreme mosquitos or other bugs can be just as worrisome. Find out when the mosquitoes or other biting insects (chiggers, black flies, etc.) are at their worst in the areas you'd like to travel to and try to avoid going at those times. Mosquitoes prefer calmer air, so park in a windy spot if they're out in force. They are most prevalent in wet areas, so avoid those when possible. Keep bug spray in your vehicle and use it when necessary. An anti-itch/anti-swelling cream or liquid is also helpful. Permethrin is a long-lasting insect repellant that can be used on clothing, tents, bug screens, or other soft items. Some sort of bug zapper or mosquito-repelling coils or candle can also work well, but I do not suggest having any flame or burning item inside your SUV.

Emergency communication

Some of the best places to travel to are also some of the most remote, and there's a good chance that your cell phone won't get reception. What are the emergency communication options when you can't call for help on your phone?

One option is a personal locating beacon, often referred to as a PLB. These are simple devices. You press a button, an emergency signal is sent out, and rescuers are notified of your position. PLBs use GPS and are not reliant on cellular networks. They are made for hikers, hunters, adventurers, travelers, pilots, boaters, and anyone else who travels to remote areas. These generally run in the $250 range, and the battery inside of them will last for five years in standby mode, after which it can be replaced. While not great for something like getting a flat tire on the side of the road (you don't want a helicopter coming to your rescue for that), one of these can literally be a lifesaver if, for example, you trip and break an ankle while hiking or your SUV breaks down in the desert in the middle of the summer and you don't have enough water.

Satellite messengers are another option. Satellite messengers transmit your location at intermittent intervals of your choice and can even track your location so that others can see your route and monitor your progress. Some allow basic one-way communication (e.g., sending a pre-written message saying that you're OK), while others allow two-way text messaging. These devices range in price from $150 to $400, and they also have fees ranging from $12 to $100 a month depending on what capabilities you want and how much you will use the device.

One step up from satellite messengers are satellite phones. These vary widely in price from $400 to $1,000 or more depending on which satellite network you use, and the various plans (i.e., prepaid, postpaid, month-to-month, etc.) also range widely in cost. This is the most expensive emergency communication option but also arguably the most useful in that you can actually talk with people as you would over a regular phone. Any of the above emergency communication devices can also be rented for the duration of your trip in a wilderness area.

Amateur radio (often called ham radio) is the final option I'll talk about here. I am not an amateur radio operator, and I know very little about the subject, but I have heard that an amateur radio can work in even very remote areas. The catch here is that they require a license to operate. There are a few tiers of licensing, and the lowest can apparently be achieved after just a week of studying. These radios range in price from around $40 for little handheld models to many hundreds and even thousands of dollars for larger (and more powerful) desktop models, depending on the size and power of the rig you want. Communicating with others via ham radio is also a practical and entertaining hobby for the SUV RVer.

With all of these options, remember that a dead battery can lead to a dead you, so make sure the device is always charged or able to be charged quickly.

Theft and break-ins

Along with breakdowns, break-ins are what I'm most afraid of when I'm on the road. I suppose there are two parts to break-ins: prevention and the cure. And you know what they say: an ounce of prevention is worth a pound of cure.

Apart from locking your doors, the best ways to prevent break-ins are to (1) park in safe areas and avoid dodgy areas, (2) hide from sight any items that look like they are worth stealing, and (3) avoid looking like you've got a ton of valuable stuff in your vehicle (because a thief might think that there's got to be something valuable in all of that stuff).

The first way is self-explanatory. The second involves keeping things like computers or tools properly stored and hidden out of sight. The third way is the trickiest because SUVs are pretty small spaces, and it usually takes a lot of stuff to live in or travel out of one. How can you hide all of that? The same way you'd hide the fact that you're sleeping in your vehicle; that is, with tinted windows, curtains, poster board in the windows, etc. If no one can see all of the tasty morsels inside your vehicle, they'll be less tempted to break in. Also, if the stuff in your vehicle is visible through your rear window, you could reduce visibility by backing into parking spaces.

I can actually lock the large plastic storage bin I have in the back of my SUV to a metal tie-down ring on the inside wall of the vehicle. When I know I'll be away from the vehicle for an extended period of time, I put valuables like my

Figure 80. A plastic storage bin chained and locked to an inside tie-out loop

laptop inside of this bin and chain it with a lock to the tie-down point. (See Figure 80.) While a motivated thief would be able to cut the lock and the chain, my hope is that seeing my setup would make the potential thief think twice before putting in the time and effort to steal my stuff.

Finally, make sure that the data on your cell phone, tablet, and laptop is backed up on the cloud so that if those items are stolen or damaged, your data is still recoverable.

A vehicle alarm may deter some thieves, though experienced ne'er-do-wells can disable them quickly. Even something that looks like a vehicle alarm may be effective. My SUV doesn't have an alarm, but it does for some reason have a blinking red light that says SECURITY above it. I'd be having serious second thoughts if I were an amateur thinking about breaking into a vehicle and saw that light blinking inside.

My guess is that the longer your SUV is parked, the higher the chances of a break-in, so avoid doing things like leaving your vehicle in parking lots or on public streets for several days.

The remoteness of your parked vehicle may also be a factor. For example, if your SUV is parked in a busy parking lot where people are constantly coming and going, a thief may be deterred by a vehicle alarm system. The thief would not want to call attention to his attempted break-in by a vehicle alarm going off. However, if you are the only vehicle parked at a remote location, a thief may not be concerned about the loud wail of a vehicle alarm system because no one would be around to hear it.

Now let's move onto the cure side of things. What can you do if your SUV is broken into and your stuff stolen? Not a whole lot. Filing a police report is the first thing you'll need to do, and the second is to call your insurance agent. If you have a lot of valuables, getting insurance on the items before you start SUV RVing is a good idea so that they can be easily replaced if they are stolen. Take pictures of and document everything in your vehicle so you can figure out what things are missing. Check your homeowner's policy too. Many cover household items that are taken from your vehicle. Check ahead with your insurance agent.

Finally, comprehensive vehicle insurance will—knock on wood—cover the cost of your vehicle if the whole thing gets stolen.

Cameras

There are a couple of different cameras that an SUV RVer could install in his or her SUV to improve safety. One is a dash cam. This forward-facing camera is mounted on the dashboard (hence the name) or from the rear view mirror, and it will record anything going on in front of your vehicle. Having this footage may be helpful for capturing an accident or vandalism. If nothing else, it can capture footage of your driving adventures. Remember that this is also another device that needs charging. If you want to record the interior of your vehicle, you can simply turn it around.

The other camera that SUV RVers might find useful is the backup camera. These cameras show you what is behind you, thus preventing accidents when backing up. Many higher-end vehicles already have these cameras installed, but they can also be aftermarket additions. This kind of camera would also be excellent if you can't see out of your rear window for whatever reason (e.g., you've got them covered, there're blocked by stuff, you're towing a trailer, etc.).

12. Long-Term SUV RVing

To see additional relevant links for this chapter, visit http://suvrving.com/book/twelve/.

It's one thing to spend a few nights in your SUV, but what if you want to spend more time on the road? What if you want to spend a month or two (or more) exploring? What if you want to live out of your SUV? There are a number of things you can do that will make your life easier, and that's what this chapter is all about.

Outdoor living areas

The biggest problem with an SUV as a tiny mobile home is lack of space. There's just not a whole lot of room to comfortably do much other than sleep or sit. But one of the best things about living—however briefly—in an SUV is that you can easily drive out to the forest, desert, mountains, lake, park, beach, or whatever other outdoor spaces you enjoy most. "Tiny house, big yard" is the idea here. You can sleep in your vehicle while doing other in-camp activities outside, and there are a number of things that will make this outdoor life more comfortable and enjoyable.

As mentioned in the section on cooking, a good awning will protect you from the sun and rain. It's great not just for cooking but also for lounging around camp or any other outdoor activity. A simple awning can be made with a cheap tarp and some cord, but fancier retractable versions that mount to your specific SUV's roof rack are commercially available. Some of these commercially available awnings have aftermarket accessories like shade or privacy walls and mosquito tents. A shade wall is helpful when the sun is lower in the sky as opposed to directly above you, but it can also be good for keeping the wind at bay. A shade wall can be made with a second tarp of similar size and more cord. A collapsible shade canopy is another option for keeping rain and sun off of you but will take up significantly more space than a tarp.

One problem I encountered when trying to set up a tarp as an awning was that the tarp was wider than the roof rack on top of my SUV was long. The rectangular tarp was five feet (1.5 meters) long on its short side (the side that I wanted to attach to the roof rack), but the length of the rack on top of my SUV

Figure 81. The initial tarp setup for my SUV, with the tarp longer than my roof rack. The right and middle grommets on the vehicle side of the tarp are tied to the roof rack. Attached to the left grommet is a long piece of cord that runs diagonally across the windshield (below the dotted line) and hooks onto the wheel rim on the far side of the SUV. The tarp is being supported by two trekking poles.

was much shorter than that. I could tie the rear corner of the tarp onto the roof rack at the rear of the vehicle and the tarp's center section to the middle of the rack, but the tarp's front corner extended out beyond the front edge of the roof rack; there was nothing I could attach the tarp's front corner to. For several outings I solved this by tying a long piece of cord to the tarp's front corner grommet, running it diagonally across the windshield, and using a carabiner as a hook to attach it to the wheel rim on the opposite side of the vehicle. (See Figure 81.)

This worked well enough, but it was kind of a pain to set up, and I didn't like that the cord was rubbing up against the windshield and the side of the SUV. I needed to find a way to extend the length of my roof rack. Figure 82 shows what I came up with.

I bought a ten-foot (three-meter) section of black 1.5-inch (3.8-centimeter) ABS plastic pipe from a local home improvement store and cut it to about five feet (1.5 meters) long (a bit longer than the width of the tarp). I then used a saw and rasp to cut out grooves or channels in the pipe so that the underside of the pipe would securely rest on top of the roof rack's crossbars. Next, I drilled holes through the pipe on both sides of each channel and secured the pipe to the roof rack crossbars using large hose clamps. I also wrapped a length of cut-up bicycle tube around each rack crossbar before mounting the pipe to make it fit

Figure 82. The black ABS pipe roof rack extension that allows tarps to be quickly attached and detached from the top of the vehicle. Locknuts and wingnuts are attached to each machine screw.

Figure 83. A diagram of the roof rack extender pipe. Note the chunks of pipe cut out to make the pipe fit more securely onto the roof rack (the two light gray areas). The three holes in the pipe are where the three outward-facing screws are placed. Large hose clamps secure the pipe to the roof rack crossbars.

Figure 84. The grommets of the tarp are placed over the screws that stick out from the pipe roof rack extender. The tarp is then pulled tight, and the opposite side of the tarp is held out by and secured to poles or trees.

more snugly and to protect the crossbar. The total cost of the project was less than $15. It can be removed in just a few minutes and put back on again in the same amount of time. (See Figure 83.)

To make setting up and taking down the tarp ultra fast and easy, I drilled three sets of holes through the sides of the pipe, placed three small-diameter machine screws through the holes so that they stick out of the pipe, and secured them with locknuts. These screws are placed along the pipe where the grommets of the tarp are located. (See Figure 81 for a full diagram.) To set up the tarp, all I have to do is slide the grommets along the side of the tarp over screws, pull the tarp tight, and secure the other end to poles, trees, etc. (See Figure 84.)

The system works perfectly, and I couldn't be happier. The pipe doesn't look amazing on top of my SUV, but it doesn't look terrible either, and it makes setting up and taking down the tarp so much faster and easier. Caps can be purchased to finish off the ends if desired to give it a custom look.

By adding wing nuts to the screws, I can attach a second tarp that extends across the SUV's roof over to the opposite side of the vehicle. This provides shade and protection from rain for the back passenger side window. (The wing nuts keep the second tarp from sliding off of the screws.) With both tarps attached, I can have the windows in both rear doors rolled all the way down

Figure 85. Two tarps covering both side windows. Both tarps attach to the pipe roof rack extender. The tarps provide rain and sun protection.

and not get any rain inside the vehicle during a storm. (See Figure 85.)

If you'll be sleeping in one place for multiple nights and the area is popular with campers, you might have trouble finding a campsite when you return in the evening after spending the day elsewhere. Leaving an inexpensive tent or a couple of chairs at the campsite is a good way to "claim" it so that no one moves in while you're away.

If mosquitoes and other insects are a problem, consider getting a bug tent or canopy that you can use outside of your tent. Some of these are large enough to fit over a picnic table. They do tend to be large and bulky when packed, so only take one if you really need it or have plenty of storage space.

A good chair is an essential piece of outdoor living equipment. There are a ton of very comfortable folding or collapsible camp chairs out there, but the trick is finding one that doesn't take up half the space in your SUV. Camping or travel chairs are specifically made to be small and portable and are great for SUV RVers. Folding stadium-style seats made for camping are small and don't take up much space, but you'll need to use them either on the ground or on top of a rock, sturdy storage bin, etc. I used to travel with an extremely comfortable collapsible chair with a built-in footrest (it was like having a recliner), but I eventually got tired of shuffling it around inside the vehicle to access other things. I replaced it with the smallest collapsible camp chair I could find and have been very happy with it. If you need something to sit on only occasionally, consider getting a small collapsible camp stool. When collapsed, these are only a couple of inches in diameter and a couple of feet long.

A table can be great for things like preparing and cooking food, playing games, and using a laptop. As with chairs, look for ones that are specifically made for camping. Folding desks made for laptop usage or for eating while on a couch can also be small and good for travel.

One aspect of outdoor living is taking things that use up a lot of space inside your SUV (e.g., food boxes, storage bins, coolers, water jugs, musical instruments, suitcases, toilets, portable solar panels, etc.) and moving them outside. This isn't practical in a parking lot, but it is practical if you have a campsite that you'll be at for at least a couple of days. Just make sure the weather forecast is good so that your stuff won't get wet when it rains.

Other items that can make outdoor living more enjoyable include lanterns, rugs or mats that you can wipe your feet on to keep the inside of your SUV clean, privacy tents for showering and going to the bathroom, and hammocks. Of course, each of these items adds to the pile of stuff you'll be taking with you, so be judicious in your packing.

Indoor living areas

If the weather is poor or if you need/want to be in an urban or suburban environment, something like a privacy tent or hammock won't be of much use. What will be useful is taking advantage of existing indoor areas to work, relax, use the restroom, read, or go online. These indoor areas include many places that I've mentioned elsewhere in the book, namely:

- Libraries
- University buildings
- Shopping malls
- Coffee shops
- Restaurants (especially fast food restaurants)
- Large bookstores
- Coworking spaces
- Gyms
- Truck stops
- Rest areas
- Community centers
- Laundromats
- Movie theaters – These are not great for hanging out, but obviously are a good place to watch movies and spend a couple of hours.

If I'm on the road for an extended period of time and need to spend a whole day working on my laptop, I'll try to move locations every few hours. I do this mostly to keep things interesting; sitting in one spot for the entire day is rough. If I'm in a large space like a library, I may just move to a different chair or table in a different part of the library.

Temporary home bases

Weeks or months of time spent on the road can wear on you. When that happens, a good idea is to find a home base for a week, month, or however long you need. There are two ways to go about this. The first is to simply set up camp in a place you like and stay put. "Stay put" here can mean either literally not move from your camp or stay in one town. You'll be able to relax and recharge without having to figure out where you're going to sleep next.

The second way to have a temporary home base is to rent one. Stay in a hotel for a few nights, or call around to find one that offers good weekly rates. Another option is to rent a room in someone's home or an entire home on Airbnb (hosts often offer discounted rates for week-long or month-long stays). I've done this many times and always had good experiences. You can recharge your batteries (both literally and figuratively), clean out your SUV, do your laundry, and plan the next leg of your adventure.

Doing laundry

If you're SUV RVing for a week or even two, you can probably pack enough clothing to avoid having to stop at a laundromat, but you'll have to wash your clothes sooner or later if you pack light or are on an extended trip. I have an extreme dislike of washing my clothing by hand, so I take my clothes to a laundromat whenever necessary. I keep my dirty clothes in a mesh bag, and I take that into the laundromat along with my laundry kit. This is a large Ziploc bag that contains laundry soap, fabric softener dryer sheets, Color Catcher sheets (these let me put both lights and darks in one load without having to worry about color bleeding), and quarters. I like the liquid laundry soap that comes in individual little square packets, but another good option is to put a load's worth of powdered laundry soap into a small, snack-sized Ziploc bag and take as many of them as necessary for the trip.

There have been a couple of times when I've washed my clothes by hand out of necessity. One time I was camping in Big Bend National Park, which is a desert park out in the middle of nowhere in West Texas. I was doing a lot of hiking and had run out of clean socks and underwear. Not wanting to leave the park and drive a long way to find a laundromat, I cut the top off of an empty one-gallon water jug, stuffed several pairs of socks and underwear inside, and filled it with soap and water. I used the handle of a hammer to act as an agitator to pound and stir the clothes around. I then transferred the dirty water into another container for later disposal (emptying soapy water onto the ground in a national park felt wrong and might be illegal) and rinsed and wrung out the clothes. I didn't have a long enough piece of rope or cord to use as a clothesline (though I made sure I had one on my next trip), so I gathered some long sticks, leaned them against logs and rocks, and draped the clothes over the sticks. Did this get the clothes as clean as they would have been if I'd washed them in a machine? No, but I was able to get them clean enough to strip them of their bad smells and keep using them.

There are a number of better ways to wash your clothes yourself. Fill a bucket with water and soap, dump your clothes in, and use a clean plunger to agitate the clothing. You can also buy devices that look like a plunger but are specifically made for washing clothes in a bucket.

Another, more compact option is to put clothes into large Ziploc bags or dry bags, add water, and knead the bags with your hands. A relatively new, more specialized device in this area is the Scrubba Wash Bag (which may or may not still be around when you read this). It is essentially a watertight bag with bumps on the inside that act the same as the ridges on a washboard. After filling the bag with water, liquid soap, and clothes, you let air out through a valve and rub or knead the bag for thirty seconds for a quick wash or three minutes for a "machine-quality" wash. The general consensus I've seen from the reviews online is that it works better than traditional hand washing but not as well as a washing machine, which makes sense to me. Because it packs down to a very small size and weighs only 5 ounces (142 grams), it is something that could be taken along in even the smallest vehicle.

There are also several small, portable, hand-powered washing machines on the market (with "small" being a relative term). These are cylindrical devices with a hand crank on the side. You load them with water, soap, and clothing and turn the crank for a couple of minutes. This spins the cylindrical main tank, causing the clothes inside to tumble around. Once you've finished cranking, you drain the water out through a spout at the bottom of the tank. Filling the tank up with clean water and cranking it again to rinse the clothes finishes off the washing process. The big problem with this type of machine is that it is bulky. It would probably only make sense to bring one of these things along on your travels if you had a very large SUV, a large rooftop/tailgate cargo box, really, really enjoyed cranking a washing machine, or had some aversion to laundromats.

You can also hand wash your clothes in a hotel room. Clean the bathroom sink, add a few items of clothing, add soap and water, let the clothes soak, agitate the clothes by rubbing and kneading them with your hands, drain the dirty water, rinse the clothes, wring out the clothes, and hang them up to dry. In a pinch I've hung clothes on hotel room shower rods, doorknobs, chairs, open cabinet doors, and open dresser drawers. If you can control the temperature in your hotel room and want the clothing to dry as quickly as possible, turn up the heat. Also, the more humid the environment, the longer the clothes will take to dry, so take this into consideration when planning your washing.

Regardless of how exactly you plan on washing your clothes yourself, make sure you have a long enough length of some sort of cord or rope to use as a clothesline. If you'll be washing your clothes often, bring a supply of clothespins too.

Staying healthy

I love traveling and sleeping in my SUV, but I can't think of many things that would be less appealing than being stuck inside of it with something like a bad cold, the flu, or diarrhea. If you do get sick while on the road, it may be worth returning home, splurging for a hotel or Airbnb room, or crashing at a friend's house until you're feeling better (assuming you have a friend that you want to do that to).

Prevention is definitely the best cure here, so be sure to wash your hands whenever possible, make liberal use of hand sanitizer, and take vitamins as necessary. A good first aid kit will help you fight against common illnesses and injuries. A good basic first aid kit may include the following:

- Pain relievers and anti-inflammatories (e.g., aspirin and ibuprofen)
- Cold medicine
- Antiobiotic cream (e.g., Neosporin, Polysporin)
- Cough drops
- Allergy medicines
- Adhesive bandages of various sizes
- Bandage wraps
- Gauze
- Medical tape
- Wet wipes
- Moleskin
- Q-tips
- Toothache cream (e.g., Orajel)
- Sunburn cream
- Burn ointment
- Anti-itch cream
- Tweezers
- Eye drops
- Anti-diarrheal medicine (e.g., Immodium, loperamide)
- Antacids (e.g., Tums, Rolaids)

Buy a commercially available first aid kit or create your own by purchasing the above items individually. Just be sure that the kit includes everything you need and that you know how to use everything. A small book on first aid wouldn't be a bad idea, either.

Eating healthy foods can be difficult while traveling or living in an SUV. It's all too easy to grab a pizza, burger, or taco for a quick, inexpensive, and (arguably) tasty bite to eat. So, plan out healthy meals and menus in advance (being sure to try out the meals before you leave home) and stick to the plan, especially if you find yourself gaining weight or feeling gross.

SUV RVing lends itself well to an active lifestyle, and my guess is that the average SUV RVer gets more exercise than the average person. Since a major focus of my mobile adventures is hiking and climbing mountains, I get plenty of exercise. Find an active activity that you enjoy doing and be sure to add it to your on-the-road routine. If the weather is bad or you don't or can't enjoy other activities, consider grabbing a gym membership.

Other stuff

Working while traveling – I know that while a lot of people would love to spend an extended period of time traveling around in their SUV, they don't have the time or money to do so. For some people who are at flexible places in their lives, working while traveling may be the solution. Certain types of jobs within fields like writing, web and graphic design, programming, marketing, teaching/tutoring, and consulting can be done from anywhere in the world as long as there is internet access. Another option is to travel to where seasonal jobs are available. Being a campground host, working the sugar beat harvest, and working temporarily at an Amazon warehouse during the peak holiday season are all popular jobs with traditional RVers, though some employers might be more hesitant to hire people living out of smaller vehicles like an SUV. The final option is to simply look in newspapers or on Craigslist for temporary jobs wherever you go.

Address issues – Where exactly are you supposed to have your mail sent while on the road? What address do you put when filling out forms? How do you get packages? The easiest method is to use a friend's or family member's address (with their permission, of course). If that won't work for you, you can rent a PO box at a local post office (and know that FedEx and UPS deliveries may not be accepted at a post office box) or private box at a UPS Store and use that as your address. Some of the private mailbox companies will forward your mail or even offer opening and scanning services. DakotaPost (*http://dakotapost.com*), MyRVmail (*https://www.myrvmail.com/*), and Mail-Link (*https://www.maillinkplus.com/*) offer these services and more in South Dakota, Florida, and Nevada, respectively. Places like banks or government agencies may not like that you don't have a physical address, but in practice this often isn't always a problem if you simply write #127 instead of PO Box 127.

If you want to order things online and be able to pick them up wherever you are, you can often have them sent to RV parks or hotels that you'll be staying at (but call ahead first). I've also heard of people sending packages as general delivery to a post office with the following format:

JOHN DOE
GENERAL DELIVERY
TOWN NAME, STATE 12345-9999

The post office will hold your package for up to 30 days. To pick it up, go to the post office and show your ID. Be sure that the zip code is for the city or town or area's main post office. The four 9's after the zip code are the extension for general delivery.

Figuring out what you need – Traveling around in an SUV for an extended period of time may sound great in theory, but the reality can be harsh. You might find it to be lonely or boring or uncomfortable. If that is the case, figure out what exactly it is that you're missing in your traveling life and add it in. If you're lonely, make the effort to get out and meet more people. If you're bored, find a hobby. If you're not sleeping well, invest in a better bed or mattress.

Feeling human – I've found that the very best ways to not feel like a burrow-dwelling animal (which you'll feel like if you just stay in your SUV all the time) are to make sure I interact with other people on a regular basis, keep myself as clean as possible, keep the inside of my SUV clean and tidy, and spend as much time as possible outside of the vehicle.

Endnotes

1. See *http://press.hotels.com/en-us/hpi/average-u-s-hotel-prices-increased-by-five-percent-in-2014/*.

2. From *http://www.blm.gov/nv/st/en/prog/recreation/camping.html*.

3. See *http://www.bloomberg.com/news/articles/2016-01-12/charging-a-smart phone-while-driving-isn-t-as-free-as-you-think*.

4. See *https://www.quora.com/How-much-gas-does-a-car-burn-per-hour-while-idling*.

5. From *https://en.wikipedia.org/wiki/Deep_cycle_battery*.

6. See *http://www.fhwa.dot.gov/byways/* for a map and full list of these roads.

About the Author

Tristan Higbee is a writer and adventurer with extensive rock climbing, mountaineering, and long-distance backpacking experience. He has lived in or traveled to more than 30 countries and has spent about a quarter of his life overseas. A linguist by training, he speaks Russian and Ukrainian and has also studied Spanish, Polish, and Chinese.

You can follow Tristan's adventures on his blog The Aloof (*http://thealoof.com*).

Other Books by the Author

Everest Pilgrim: A Solo Trek to Nepal's Everest Base Camp and Beyond

Himalayan Pilgrim: A Chronicle of Independent Trekking Through Nepal's Less-Traveled Regions

Annapurna Pilgrim: A Solo Trek of Nepal's Annapurna Circuit in Winter

101 Rock Climbing Tips and Tricks

***

If you found this book helpful, please leave a review on Amazon. Reviews are tremendously beneficial for independent authors and go a long way toward making affordable books possible.

The author hopes you found this book useful and that you've been inspired to have your own SUV RVing adventures. Be sure to check out the SUV RVing website and blog (*http://SUVRVing.com*) for gear recommendations and reviews, trip reports, camp locations, videos, and more. You can also contact the author there if you have questions, comments, corrections, or suggestions.

Made in the USA
Middletown, DE
08 January 2020